CULTURES OF THE WORLD

Portugal

Cavendish Square
New York

Published in 2016 by Cavendish Square Publishing, LLC
243 5th Avenue, Suite 136, New York, NY 10016
Copyright © 2016 by Cavendish Square Publishing, LLC

Third Edition

Website: cavendishsq.com

This publication represents the opinions and views of the author based on his or her personal experience, knowledge, and research. The information in this book serves as a general guide only. The author and publisher have used their best efforts in preparing this book and disclaim liability rising directly or indirectly from the use and application of this book.

CPSIA Compliance Information: Batch #CS16CSQ

All websites were available and accurate when this book was sent to press.

Library of Congress Cataloging-in-Publication Data
Names: Heale, Jay. | Koh, Angeline, 1982- | Schmermund, Elizabeth.
Title: Portugal / Jay Heale, Angeline Koh, and Elizabeth Schmermund.
Description: New York : Cavendish Square Publishing, [2016] | Series:
Cultures of the world | Includes bibliographical references and index.
Identifiers: LCCN 2015041809 | ISBN 9781502616937 (library bound) | ISBN
9781502616944 (ebook)
Subjects: LCSH: Portugal—Juvenile literature.
Classification: LCC DP517 .H4 2016 | DDC 946.9--dc23
LC record available at http://lccn.loc.gov/2015041809

Writers: Jay Heale, Angeline Koh, and Elizabeth Schmermund
Editorial Director: David McNamara
Editor: Kristen Susienka
Copy Editor: Nathan Heidelberger
Art Director: Jeffrey Talbot
Designer: Alan Sliwinski
Senior Production Manager: Jennifer Ryder-Talbot
Production Editor: Renni Johnson
Photo Research: J8 Media

Printed in the United States of America

CONTENTS

PORTUGAL TODAY

FOR NINE HUNDRED YEARS, PORTUGAL HAS REINVENTED ITSELF while keeping a complex and distinct culture. Located on the Iberian Peninsula in southwest Europe, Portugal's relatively small size contains a surprising mixture of different styles of architecture, scenery, and cuisine. Even the country's name, Portugal, reveals the layers of its rich history. Originally called Cale by the Celts, the Romans conquered the land and named it Portus Cale, or "Port of Cale." In the Dark Ages, the conquering Visigoths renamed the region Portucale. Finally, due to both Spanish and Moorish influences, "Portugal" was inaugurated in the eleventh and twelfth centuries. Other place names in Portugal reveal the similarly complex history of the region, from the Arabic Almodôvar to the Celtic Ebora, which is the modern-day city of Évora.

Portugal was once the most powerful seafaring nation in the world. During the Age of Discovery, from the fifteenth to eighteenth centuries, Portuguese explorers like Bartolomeu Dias and Vasco da Gama traveled the world's oceans on majestic ships. They established Portugal's power with colonies in South America, Africa, Asia, and Oceania, bringing their language and culture with them. But a series

Demonstrators shout during a May Day protest in Portugal in 2015.

of military defeats and a natural disaster in 1755 weakened the country and led Portugal to close its doors to outside influence and economic modernization. The once mighty country succumbed to increasing poverty and a dictatorship that lasted until 1974, when it was toppled by the democratic Carnation Revolution.

Following the revolution, Portugal entered a period of modernization. The traditional role of the family began to shift, women entered the workforce in larger numbers, and the influence of the Catholic Church steadily declined.

While the Portuguese have kept their unique traditions, they have also begun to adopt new ways of living. In 1986, Portugal joined other European nations in what would eventually be known as the European Union (EU).

This ushered in a new period of economic prosperity and opened Portugal's frontiers to international business opportunities.

Since then, Portugal has experienced highs and lows. It remains a country of arresting beauty, gentle people, and good living. However, it has struggled amid the economic recessions that have hit many countries after 2008, and received an economic bailout in 2011 from the EU and the International Monetary Fund. While unemployment remains high in Portugal today, the country endures as a beacon of beauty and easy living; tourists continue to flock to Portugal for its fine wine, delicious cuisine, and awe-inspiring sights.

The beautiful coastline of Madeira.

GEOGRAPHY

The Iberian Peninsula comprises the nations of Spain, Portugal, and Andorra.

1

PORTUGAL'S VAST EMPIRE WAS THE first and longest-lasting colonial empire in Europe. Its conquests began during the explorations by Portuguese sailors along the coast of Africa in the early 1400s and lasted until Portugal granted East Timor sovereignty in 2002. This small, rectangular country in the southwestern corner of the Iberian Peninsula once governed colonies in South America, Africa, India, Oceania (East Timor), and China. While the Portuguese empire is a fraction of the size it once was, its legacy endures; today Portuguese is the sixth most widely spoken language in the world, with approximately 240 million speakers.

"Oh salty sea, how much of your salt are tears of Portugal!" —Portuguese Poet Fernando Pessoa in "Mar Português"

Portugal is about the size of the state of Indiana. It covers 35,556 square miles (92,090 square kilometers) and is home to 10.5 million people. Its coastline stretches 1,114 miles (1,793 kilometers). Portugal includes two autonomous regions, the Azores and Madeira archipelagos, which are all that remain of Portugal's once extensive empire. Located off the coast of Portugal in the Atlantic Ocean, these islands are home to approximately five hundred thousand people, mostly of Portuguese descent.

Mainland Portugal is divided into two types of administrative regions: metropolitan areas and inter-municipal communities. The metropolitan areas of Portugal are further divided into the areas including and surrounding the large cities of Lisbon and Porto. As of 2015, there are twenty-one inter-municipal communities, which include the northern regions of Douro, Alto Minho, and Terras de Trás-os-Montes; the central regions of Alto Alentejo, Região de Coimbra, and Região de Leiria; and the southern regions of Baixo Alentejo and Algarve.

CLIMATE

The northern regions are often mountainous with rocky terrain of schist, granite, and slate. Summers are hot and dry, while winters are wet and cold, but Lisbon's mean average temperature lies in the range of 60 to 65 degrees Fahrenheit (15.6 to 18.3 degrees Celsius). The climate and geography of the

The Serra da Estrela Mountains covered in fresh snow.

PORTO

The name Porto means simply "Port." Foreigners sometimes call the city Oporto, a misunderstanding stemming from Portuguese references to o porto, or "the port." In Roman times, the area nearby was called Portucale, which became the name of the kingdom and then of the country. Porto assumed the title of "The Unconquered City" due to its residents' courage in fighting off the Moors and later the armies of Napoleon.

Porto is a busy commercial city with prosperity and poverty existing side by side. Home to the port wine trade, it is built on steep hills on the northern bank of the Douro River. The river is spanned by two spectacular bridges. The single-span rail bridge was designed by Gustave Eiffel, the architect of Paris's Eiffel Tower. The two-tiered Dom Luís road bridge joins the commercial city center with the southern bank of the Douro.

central region (between the Douro and Tejo Rivers) are more diverse. Small- to medium-sized farms, as well as the country's mining and light industries, share the land with pine forests and dunes. Southern Portugal (Alto and Baixo Alentejo, and Algarve) is a dry and warm agricultural area. Plantations of cork oaks and olive trees are grown in the undulating plains.

Hot, dry summers and short, mild winters are normal for most of the central areas. The western coastline enjoys cool evening breezes. Westerly winds and the surrounding waters provide much of Portugal with cool, damp weather in the winter months of December and January, although inland the northern mountains of Serra da Estrela can get snow. The average annual rainfall is 46 inches (116.8 centimeters) in the northwestern vine-growing country and 27 inches (68.5 cm) in the capital city of Lisbon. The inland plains receive virtually no rain through the summer months.

THE NORTHERN REGION

Northern Portugal is divided into northeastern and northwestern regions. The capital of the Região Norte, as it is known, is Porto, which is the second-largest city in Portugal and the city that gives its name to the most famous wine of the country—port. The northwestern region is densely populated and industrialized, while the northeastern region is more rural and mountainous.

The Douro River flows from northern Spain to Porto. The Douro River Valley has long been a special place for growing wine, which was traditionally taken down river on flat-bottom boats from various vineyards to the city of Porto. This is how port—the sweet wine that can only be produced in the Douro region—received its name. The rich soil of this region is also excellent for the cultivation of grapes that

The Braga Cathedral dates back to the fifteenth century.

produce the white wine called *vinho verde*, or young, green wine. Terraces have been cut out of the steep green hillsides to produce these grapes, which overlook the Minho, Lima, and Cávado Rivers.

A major town in the northwest region is Braga, whose narrow primary street leads past old-fashioned shop fronts, with tiny ironwork balconies, to its huge Romanesque cathedral. The palace of the archbishop of Braga houses one of the largest libraries in the country. The mountain town of Guimarães, another important city in the region, is known as the birthplace of Portugal. From here, Afonso Henriques, the country's first king, launched his defeat of the Moors, who had all but overrun the land. To the north, near the Spanish border, the woods of Serra do Gerês, rich with oak, quince, cedar, chestnut, pine, and maple, are popular for walking.

To the northeast lies a mountainous region that the Portuguese call the Trás-os-Montes, meaning "beyond the mountains". The mountain ranges there are extensions of the Cantabrian Mountains of northwestern Spain. The winters in the mountains can be fiercely cold, and the summer months are hot and dry. Villages in these mountain regions retain their medieval appearance, and stone mileposts provide frequent evidence of Roman occupation. The countryside is covered with rolling hills, and olive groves crowd the riverbanks.

The rivers of Trás-os-Montes feed into several hydroelectric dams, and these have brought irrigation to the arid soils of this province. It is a rural area with poor soil and hard-won crops of rye and potatoes. However, the region is making slow but steady progress with aid provided by the EU. There are many spas here where visitors "take the cure" with underground mineral waters rich with fluoride and bicarbonate of soda. One of the more popular spas is at Chaves. There are vineyards as well. At the town of Vila Real is an ornate building that serves as the headquarters for producers of the world-famous Mateus Rosé wine.

A colorful spring landscape in Portugal.

Nazaré is one of the most famous surfing destinations in the world.

The Serra da Estrela is a great mountain barrier in the center of Portugal. It is the country's tallest mountain chain and contains Estrela, the nation's highest point at 6,532 feet (1,991 meters). Corn and rye grow in the valleys of this chain. The villagers weave woolen goods, make sheep's-milk cheese, and raise pigs. Covilhã has become a winter sports center, although hiking on trails in the mountains may be an even more popular tourist attraction.

THE COSTA DE PRATA

The main Atlantic coastline between Lisbon and Porto is known as the Costa de Prata, or Silver Coast. The area is rich with history, made richer by tourism. The traditional fishing village of Nazaré has grown into an over-decorated tourist trap, where fishing boats are garishly painted and the locals wear traditional clothing to earn tips. Fishermen used to roll their boats across the

A view of the university city of Coimbra from Clara Bridge.

beach on wooden rollers. They would then row out to sea, drop their nets, and use teams of oxen to haul the nets in. Today, tractors and cranes make the fishing trade more efficient and less romantic.

The town of Aveiro is situated on a saltwater lagoon of the Vouga River delta and is crisscrossed by canals spanned by humpbacked bridges. It is nicknamed the Portuguese Venice. Also in this region is the walled town of Óbidos, a bridal gift from the king of Portugal, Dinis, to his queen, Elizabeth. The region contains the pilgrimage town of Fátima and the town of Tomar with its fortified castle built by the great crusading Order of the Knights Templar.

Coimbra, an ancient university town with narrow, cobbled streets, was founded by the Romans and occupied by the Moors until the eleventh century. It was the capital of Portugal in the twelfth and thirteenth centuries, as well as the seat of power of a Roman Catholic bishop. It boasts one of Europe's oldest universities.

LISBON

The capital city of Lisbon is the oldest city in Western Europe. Known as "The City of Seven Hills" and "Queen of the Sea," legend holds that the Greek hero Ulysses founded Lisbon on his return home from Troy. Its Roman influence can still be seen today in the black and white pavement that crisscrosses the pedestrian areas of the city. The ten towers of the Castle of Saint George dominate the center of the capital and overlook the Tejo River. At the heart of the city stands the grand Praça do Comércio, or the Square of Commerce, a wide plaza that once opened to the ancient royal palace and is now surrounded by eighteenth-century government buildings.

Much of the oldest architecture of Lisbon no longer exists. That's because on November 1, 1755, an earthquake struck Lisbon, killing forty thousand

This illustration shows the destroyed city of Lisbon following the earthquake of 1755.

residents and destroying 85 percent of its structures. The Ribeira Palace, once home to the Portuguese royal family, collapsed; it stood where the Praça do Comércio stands today. Following the earthquake, the city center was reconstructed under the guidance of Prime Minister Sebastião José de Carvalho e Melo, otherwise known as the Marquis de Pombal. His goal was to rebuild the city according to modern urban planning of the time, and thus, he destroyed any remaining older structures to make way for his vision of a modern, mid-eighteenth-century Lisbon.

Eighteenth-century buildings surround modern-day Commerce Square in Lisbon.

THE ALENTEJO IN VERSE

All is so calm and chaste, so like a dream.
That looking at this masterpiece of God, I ask myself
Where is there a painter, an artist so supreme,
So profoundly wise as to unfurl
A canvas with a more arresting scene,
More delicate and beautiful in this world?
—Florbela Espanca, Portuguese poet

To the west of Lisbon lies Sintra, once the summer retreat of the Portuguese kings. The riverside area of Belém is the port from which large Portuguese trading ships once set off. At this place is the impressive Monastery of Jerónimos, built in memory of the famous explorer Vasco da Gama and his successful journey to India in 1499.

THE PLAINS OF THE ALENTEJO

The spreading plains of central and southern Portugal are collectively called the Alentejo, meaning "beyond the Tejo River." The province is divided into two: Alto (Upper) Alentejo and Baixo (Lower) Alentejo. This area occupies a third of the total land area of Portugal and is covered with fields of wheat, oats, rice, grapes, and tomatoes. Cork oaks and olive trees grow everywhere. The land is dotted with white farmhouses, prehistoric stone circles, and occasional trees, which do not prevent it from scorching to a burnt brown in the hot summer months. The only shade for sheep and black pigs is in the large plantations of cork oaks.

Rural Alentejo was the heart of popular support for Portuguese communism. Great farming estates were taken over by the workers during the 1974 revolution, but they failed financially from a succession of poor harvests. Now many of the original owners are buying their land back and

The sparse Alentejo countryside in Castro Verde.

introducing new farming methods that will increase productivity and help reap better profits.

The main city is Évora, with a population of fifty-six thousand. It is an educational and cultural center that is the country's fifth most important town after Lisbon, Porto, Coimbra, and Guimarães. Moorish alleyways, a Roman temple, a Gothic cathedral, and the several Renaissance palaces in the city make it somewhat like a museum town.

THE SOUTHERN ALGARVE

The thin strip of Portugal's southern beaches got its name from the Arabic *al-gharb* ("the west"). A local legend tells of a Moorish king who captured a bride from the north. When she pined for the snow of her homeland and became ill, he planted almond trees, and the white blossoms both cured her and convinced her of his love.

The limestone cliffs of Marinha cove in Algarve.

A mallard duck flies near a traditional Portuguese fishing boat in the Tejo estuary.

Long, sandy beaches between rocky coves, together with a rain-free Mediterranean summer climate, have made the Algarve one of the prime tourist destinations of Europe. Situated almost centrally along this southern coastline, the town of Faro acts as a tourist center and airport. The ancient port of Lagos, from which Portuguese fleets and navigators used to sail, still has the arcades of its old slave market. To the west are tiny bays, often with eroded rocks and picturesque grottoes. One of the most famous is Praia da Rocha with its strange outcrops of red and yellow sandstone.

PLANT AND ANIMAL LIFE

Portugal's birdlife is pleasantly varied because the country is on a main migratory route. Algarve fishermen often see dunlins from Iceland, and Alentejo children greet flocks of azure-winged magpies or crested hoopoes. White egrets follow the plough, and storks nest on many a bell tower. Eagles, falcons, kestrels, storks, and vultures hover over the northern mountains. There are even flamingos in the Tejo estuary. Madeira claims wildlife fame for its 695 species of beetles!

European field animals, such as rabbits, hares, badgers, and foxes, are common in Portugal. The civet cat still roams despite being shot at often by people for raiding poultry yards. In Peneda-Gerês National Park in the far north, there are deer, boars, lynxes, and a few remaining wolves, and the nearly extinct Luso-Galician ponies run wild and free in the park. There are national breeds of dogs: the handsome Serra da Estrela, the pointer Perdigueiro (once a hunting dog), and the curious Cão d'Agua, or "water dog." The water dog is a unique breed of dog that slightly resembles a poodle. It is large and muscular, with curly hair that is either black and white or brown

THE IBERIAN LYNX

The Iberian lynx is the world's most endangered feline. Weighing on average 28 pounds (13 kilograms), this fierce cat has tufted ears, long hair on its chin that resembles a beard, and spotted fur. This species of lynx once inhabited the entire Iberian Peninsula, but since its main source of food—rabbits—has become more scarce and as humans take over the lynx's land, its population has decreased rapidly.

Portuguese conservationists are trying to reverse the Iberian lynx's worrisome decline. In 2014, two Iberian lynxes were released into the Guadiana Valley Nature Park in southeastern Portugal—the first time an Iberian lynx has ever been released into the wild in Portugal. This followed the creation of the National Pact for the Conservation of the Iberian Lynx, a document signed by researchers and landowners promising to take measures to save this beautiful creature. Conservationists plan to release more Iberian lynxes and to provide protected land for these creatures so that they can thrive. Due in part to these conservation efforts, the Iberian lynx has recently been changed from a critically endangered species to an endangered species in recent years.

and white, webbed feet for better swimming, and a tail that is curved up over its back and serves as a rudder. It can swim as far as 5 miles (8 km), carrying messages between boats, and dive 12 feet (3.7 m) deep to pull up fish and nets. Water dogs bark warnings in a fog and even save people from drowning. They are, however, increasingly rare.

Portugal's floral kingdom is particularly rich, with over 2,700 species of wildflowers. From February to June, the southern coastal regions blaze with rock roses, anemones, celandines, thrift, and vetch. The inland scrubland is scented with herbs such as rosemary, thyme, and lavender and is colorful with irises, lupines, and scarlet poppies. Arum lilies grow wild in marshy areas. Flowering rhododendrons and oleander bushes grow in many of the woodlands, and the dark green, leathery carob bean tree grows in the south. Sweet basil is found everywhere.

Horta, a small town on Faisal Island in the Azores.

AUTONOMOUS REGIONS OF PORTUGAL

The archipelagos, or island chains, of the Azores and Madeira are Portuguese territories. They are, however, autonomous regions with their own legislatures and governments. Both islands were discovered through Henry the Navigator's expeditions in the early 1400s and colonized shortly after. Today, both island chains are popular tourist destinations, although the Madeira Islands have been developed into resorts while the Azores are better known for their more undeveloped natural beauty.

THE AZORES This group of nine islands has a total area of 922 square miles (2,388 sq km) and a population of 255,000. They lie in a strategic position—in the North Atlantic Ocean, off the western coast of Africa, about 1,000 miles (1,600 km) from Lisbon. The climate is temperate, with plenty of rain. Volcanic hot springs abound, and extinct craters have created spectacular lakes and bays. Cattle and dairy products, in addition to fish, support the islanders. Legend has it that these islands are the tips of the lost continent of Atlantis, sunk centuries ago by a great volcanic upheaval.

THE MADEIRA ISLANDS Located in the North Atlantic Ocean about 535 miles (856 km) southwest of Lisbon and 350 miles (560 km) off the northwestern coast of Africa, the Madeira Islands consist of two large islands and several uninhabited islets with a total area of 314 square miles (813 sq km) and a population of 268,000.

It is said that sailors once lit a fire to clear space among the thick forests in the islands. The blaze went out of control and burned for seven years. Whether this is true or not, the fact remains that the thick tree growth on the group of islands gave it the name Madeira, meaning "wood." Today, the Madeira Islands have terraced fields climbing up sheer mountainsides. Plagued by pirates in the eighteenth century, disease in its vineyards in the nineteenth century, and floods and economic slumps more recently, Madeira nonetheless remains a beautiful place to live.

A woman named Mrs. Phelps took samples of Madeira embroidery to London in the nineteenth century, and this started a major export industry. The most famous local product is the nutty, spicy Madeira wine.

"The Azores, along with the archipelagos of Madeira, Canary Islands and Cape Verde, constitute the biogeographic region of Macaronesia, a name which means 'fortunate islands' for those who live there and visit them."
—VisitAzores.com

INTERNET LINKS

www.algarvewildlife.com
This online guide offers information on wildlife and habitats in Portugal's Algarve region.

www.britannica.com/place/Portugal
This is a comprehensive site on Portugal, including information on its geography and various climates.

www.visitportugal.com/en
You can find travel information on this official Portuguese tourism website.

www.worldatlas.com/webimage/countrys/europe/pt.htm
This travel site has an introduction to Portugal and some of its highlights.

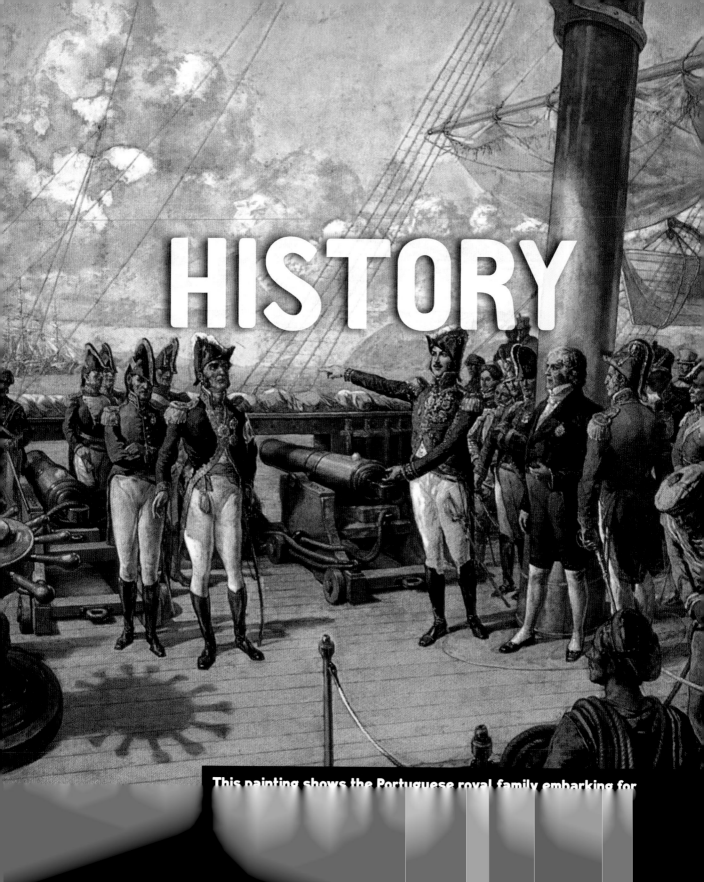

HISTORY

This painting shows the Portuguese royal family embarking for

2

L ONG BEFORE THE GOLDEN AGE OF Portugal and the Age of Discovery, the land that would become Portugal was settled, conquered, and then reconquered by various groups of people. The Celtic people and then the Romans established settlements within the modern borders of Portugal before being invaded by the Visigoths and then the Moors.

The history of modern Portugal begins in the fifteenth and sixteenth centuries, when the country created the first global empire that would stretch across half the known world. When the earthquake of 1755 destroyed Lisbon, considered the greatest European city at the time, many intellectuals and artists were stunned and devastated. In fact, the French writer and philosopher Voltaire was inspired by the great Lisbon earthquake to write his famous novel *Candide* in 1759. The Portuguese are proud of their history, and for good reason. That such a grandiose past should belong to such a small country is part of the wonder of Portugal.

ANCIENT PORTUGAL

There are dozens of abandoned stone-walled settlements in the northern hills of Portugal. Dating back to almost 1000 BCE, these were the villages of the Celtic people, or Celt-Iberians, who lived as fiercely independent tribes. In the south, Phoenician sailors set up trading stations. They were followed by the Carthaginians from North Africa. The Iberian Peninsula later became part of the Roman Empire.

Most of central and southern Portugal was included in the province the Romans named Lusitania, after a Celtic tribe that had proved tough to subdue. Although the Romans did not develop Lusitania as much as they did their other conquered regions, they did build roads and bridges and introduce wheat, barley, and grapevines. In the fourth century, the Romans brought Christianity to Portugal. After the fall of the Roman Empire, the Christian Visigoths overran Portugal. The Visigoths were a Germanic tribe that had conquered large swaths of land in France before sweeping into the Iberian Peninsula. They ruled their large kingdom effectively; in fact, their code of law became the basis of Spanish law up until the Middle Ages.

In 711 CE, the Muslim invasion began. Musa ibn Nusayr, the Muslim governor of North Africa, attacked the peninsula and killed Rodrigo, the last of the Visigoth kings. Encouraged by this success, he returned two years later with an army of eighteen thousand men.

The Moors, as the Muslim conquerors were known, swept through Spain as well but chose to settle in the southern part of Portugal, where the sunny Algarve region was much to their liking. It took Portugal five centuries to win the region back.

The next three hundred years saw constant fighting between the Christians and the Moors, who were mainly Muslims, although some were probably Coptic Christians. In the early eleventh century, King Afonso VI of Castile (in Spain) invited Henry of Burgundy to bring his crusaders to assist in forcing back the Moors. As a reward, Henry received Afonso's daughter Teresa's hand in marriage, as well as the territory between the Douro and Minho Rivers, then called Portucale, which had already been won back from the Moors. Henry and Teresa's son, Afonso Henriques (1109—1185), set out to create a kingdom for himself. He intended to do so by defeating the forces loyal to his mother, who had governed Portugal after her husband's death in 1112. He succeeded and eventually crowned himself Afonso I, the first king of Portugal, in 1139. His well-fortified castle at Guimarães became the historic cradle of Portugal.

In 1143, Portugal was accepted as a separate kingdom by its neighbors, Castile and León, and four years later, Portuguese soldiers seized Lisbon from the Moors. When Afonso I died, most of northern and central Portugal was under his control. His heirs spent the next one-and-a-half centuries fighting for southern Portugal. Following years of rival claims to the Portuguese throne, the reign of the poet-king Dinis (1261–1325) brought peace, prosperity, and a growth of culture. He also established two universities: in Lisbon in 1290 and in Coimbra in 1307. He had fifty fortresses built along the frontier with Castile, and he signed a treaty of friendship with England that was to prove vital in the years ahead.

Powerful Castile cast greedy eyes on Portugal, a country weakened in the 1340s by the pervasive and devastating plague known as the Black Death. In the decisive Battle of Aljubarrota in 1385, King João I, the first in a new line of kings, defeated the Castilians with the aid of archers sent from England. Portugal's independence was secured.

THE AGE OF DISCOVERY

King Alfonso I (1109–1185), circa 1150.

The Age of Discovery, an important period of time in European history where nations set out across oceans to discover and conquer lands, began with the Portuguese discovery of the Azores in the early fifteenth century. Thus began the golden age of Portugal, a time when this small sliver of the Iberian Peninsula became the most powerful nation on Earth. After discovering the Azores, captains sailing for Prince Henry the Navigator discovered and colonized Madeira, then the Cape Verde Islands and the Gulf of Guinea off the western coast of Africa. In 1487, Bartolomeu Dias circumnavigated the African continent when he rounded the Cape of Good Hope, the southern tip of Africa.

When Christopher Columbus, sailing under the Spanish flag, went west and discovered the American continents, the pope ruled that the unknown world was to be divided between Spain and Portugal. Spain was to have the lands west of an imaginary line west of the Cape Verde Islands, while

Portugal would have the undiscovered world east of that line—an empire that was to include Brazil, and Macau on the Chinese coast.

Portuguese exploration continued during the fifteenth and sixteenth centuries, and they were the first Westerners in Ceylon, Sumatra, Malacca, Timor, and the Moluccas; the first Europeans to trade with China and Japan; and the first explorers to see Australia. Although the Portuguese caravels (speedy sailing ships) led by Vasco da Gama had sailed as far as India in 1498, it was Portuguese navigator Ferdinand Magellan (whose voyage was sponsored by Spain) who first circumnavigated the globe.

Statue of Prince Henry the Navigator in Sagres, Portugal.

UNION WITH SPAIN AND INDEPENDENCE

Portugal faced a crisis with its monarchy in 1580 when its last two kings—King Sebastian and King Henry—died without heirs. This left the Portuguese throne vulnerable to outside attack, which is exactly what happened. King Philip II of Spain swept in to annex Portugal, whose army was destroyed in a disastrous battle in Morocco that left King Sebastian dead. The Iberian Union, as Spain's annexation of Portugal was called, lasted until it was overthrown in 1640 by the ambitious Duke of Bragança, who became King João IV (1604—1656). His daughter Catherine married King Charles II of England (1630—1685) and, as a wedding gift, England provided ten warships and two regiments each of cavalry and infantry to Portugal. This massive wedding gift provided Portugal with the means to remain independent from Spain.

The discovery of gold and diamonds in the Portuguese colony of Brazil brought new wealth to Lisbon and restructured the economy. King João V (1689—1750) embarked on several ambitious projects despite threats from the Catholic Church. The king made his own decisions and seldom called his *cortes* (kor-TEZ), or parliament, to meet. He was succeeded by his son, Joseph Emmanuel (1714—1777), or José I. José I did not share his father's passion for power and left the job of ruling Portugal to his secretary, the Marquis de Pombal. Under Pombal, Portugal's trade in port, wine, sugar, and tobacco

The third son of King João I, Prince Henry headed the expedition that sent Portuguese ships probing the farthest seas of the world. On the rocky peninsula of Sagres in the Algarve, he lived austerely as a monk for years. Working with navigators, mapmakers, and astronomers, his greatest objective was to find a sea route from Europe to the East. His team of experts improved the instruments of navigation, taught sailors to find their position by the stars, and redesigned the caravel so it could sail against the wind.

The earliest voyages to Madeira and Cape Bojador, south of the Canary Islands, were financed by the prince himself. Later, societies were formed to send Portuguese expeditions ever farther, yet these returned richer in knowledge than wealth.

The Monument to the Discoveries, at Belém (near the seaward side of Lisbon), was erected to mark the five hundredth anniversary of the death of Prince Henry. It depicts a stylized caravel bearing thirty-three human figures that represent people linked with the voyages of Portuguese discoveries; the figure of Prince Henry dominates them all.

flourished, leading to new economic stability. The country's tax and education systems were reformed and secularized with the abolishment of the Jesuit Order, which had monopolized the education systems in most Catholic countries. Slavery was banned. Pombal, however, displayed a dictatorial ruthlessness, putting to death some of his opponents who were part of the old aristocracy. This earned him a great number of enemies, the greatest of which was the Catholic Church, a powerful institution at that time.

Disaster struck on the morning of All Saints' Day, November 1, 1755. Lisbon was hit by a massive earthquake, which also generated large tsunamis. Buildings collapsed, fires raged, and between thirty thousand and forty thousand people died. However, even this grand devastation did not

The Marquis de Pombal in 1770.

daunt the competent Pombal, who set about rebuilding the city. He adopted a rational mode of action in the reconstruction of Lisbon: "Bury the dead; feed the living." Nonetheless, despite the great benefits he brought to his country and the contributions he made, Pombal was stripped of his power after the accession of Maria I (1734—1816), and many of his measures were made invalid.

In 1807, the generals of Napoleon invaded Portugal, which had allied with Britain against France. Although British troops were sent to help, the Portuguese royal family fled to Brazil. After the battle of Buçaco, in which the French lost five thousand troops, the British general Wellington withdrew his forces behind the Torres Vedras line, which had been built to defend Lisbon, and the French troops eventually retreated as well. In 1815, Wellington defeated Napoleon in a final battle at Waterloo in Belgium. King João VI returned after fourteen years in Brazil to a wild welcome from the population.

THE BIRTH OF THE REPUBLIC

King João VI (1767—1826) returned to a very different Portugal in 1821, after being crowned king in Brazil. In 1820, revolution had broken out. The revolutionaries had one main request: a constitutional monarchy with an assembly that would create Portugal's laws, elected by adult male citizens. Not all Portuguese agreed, however, and political fighting broke out. The revolutionaries demanded that King João return from Brazil, and so he did. Once back home, he accepted the terms of the radicals to keep his crown and agreed to a new constitution that was drawn up in 1822. This wasn't the end of Portugal's problems, however. Following King João's death in 1826, his son Dom Pedro, who ruled Brazil, returned to Portugal to prevent his brother Dom Miguel from seizing the throne. Dom Miguel wanted absolute power as king, and Dom Pedro battled Miguel and won, but died soon after in 1834.

Two political groups vied for power: royalists wanted the monarchy to retain absolute power, while liberalists pushed for a constitutional monarchy, more voting rights, and less power in the hands of the monarchy. Meanwhile, Portugal was nearly bankrupt and heavily in debt, with the largest amount owed to Britain, then the world's most powerful trading nation. In 1892, the Portuguese government declared itself bankrupt, and mass emigration began. The Portuguese relocated at a rate of forty thousand per year to Brazil, the colonies, and the United States.

Feeling that the king had allowed the honor of Portugal to be stained, the newly formed Republican Party urged that Portugal should become a republic, with elected government officials. King Carlos I appointed a reformist, João Franco, as premier. Franco dismissed parliament and threw his political opponents into jail or had them deported. In retaliation, the Republicans launched a military takeover in 1908. The coup failed, and the royal government reacted harshly. Although Franco was the intended target, King Carlos I and his heir were assassinated by mistake during the accompanying violence.

João VI of Portugal, circa 1818.

The successor of King Carlos I, King Manuel II, was received sympathetically, but unstable conditions prevented him from carrying out his duties. Before long, revolution was in the air. On October 4, 1910, Republican ships sailed up the Tejo to Lisbon. They bombarded the palace, while sympathetic troops and civilians held the Rotunda. King Manuel II sailed off on his royal yacht into exile in England. The Portuguese Republic was born.

THE FIRST PORTUGUESE REPUBLIC

The First Portuguese Republic lasted for sixteen years, from the 1910 revolution to 1926. During this time, there were many changes to the government. In fact, in just sixteen years there were forty-five different governments and nine presidents. It was described as a period of anarchy, where there were civil wars, monarchist insurrections, and even military

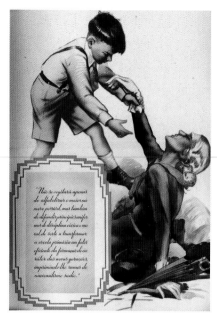

Propaganda from the New State.

coups and political assassinations. When World War I (1914—1918) broke out, Britain was short of ships and asked Portugal for assistance. In February 1916, Portugal seized German ships sheltering in what had been, until then, neutral Portuguese ports. The Portuguese public was divided over the decision to enter into the war, and political turmoil increased at home. Due in part to this, a period of dictatorships lasted until 1926. In May of that year, the Portuguese military grabbed political power and ended the First Republic.

THE NEW STATE

While the First Republic was unstable, corrupt, and even violent at times, it attempted a democratic rule of government. This was not the case for the Second Republic. When General Óscar Carmona led the military coup that overthrew the government in 1926, he declared himself president of Portugal soon after and named António de Oliveira Salazar minister of finance. Salazar became the real ruler of the country and instituted an authoritarian regime that lasted until 1974.

Salazar became prime minister in 1932, and the following year, a new constitution proclaimed the *Estado Novo* (es-TA-do NOH-vo), or New State, in which the power of the state was increased and political parties were replaced by the National Union.

Salazar had complete control over the country's finances, and his strict budget controls and reformed taxation brought financial stability. A countrywide improvement of roads, harbors, airports, and hospitals began. Dams and bridges were built, and agricultural methods were updated.

However, he ruled as a dictator and set up a secret police force that repressed any opposition to his government. Tight censorship and surveillance prevented anti-Salazar views from reaching the public.

When World War II (1939—1945) broke out, Salazar succeeded in keeping Portugal neutral. Salazar later allowed Britain to use naval and air bases on the Azores. The Portuguese people were largely anti-Nazi. Portugal thus became a safe destination for political and religious refugees fleeing Nazi Germany.

The prime minister of Portugal from 1932 to 1968, Salazar was a quiet professor of economics from Coimbra University who achieved what seemed an impossible task: that of rebuilding Portugal into a country with a stable government and a reliable economy.

From a skilled economist admired for his honesty and genius, Salazar became a relentless, autocratic dictator during the thirty-six years of his rule. He showed his authoritarian ways in his complete control of government and departmental expenditure. Nothing was to be spent without his approval. In his manipulation of politics, there was little debate. Cabinet ministers were rarely called to council meetings. Deeply influenced by religious and political ideology, he admired the order in fascist states but derided the violence. In 1936, he started a paramilitary youth brigade compulsory for all boys between the ages of eleven and fourteen. It used the Nazi salute and was modeled in part on the Hitler Youth (Hitler Jugend). A similar organization for girls was soon created.

In 1968, Salazar fell from his chair, suffered a stroke, and was removed from power. He died on July 27, 1970, believing to the end that he had kept Portugal "proudly alone."

After the war, Salazar triumphed as president in the presidential election of 1958. Many, however, claimed it was a result of electoral fraud. Salazar refused to grant Angola, Mozambique, or Guinea-Bissau independence, although in 1961, Portugal was unable to prevent India from seizing Goa.

THE PEOPLE'S REPUBLIC

After Salazar's death, Dr. Marcello Caetano, a former member of Salazar's government and a scholar, became prime minister of Portugal. Caetano attempted to pass economic and political reforms, and for a short time, the Portuguese economy seemed to improve. However, his reforms were not enough, and they came too late. Due to a lack of political support for Caetano, military forces attempted to overthrow the government. They were unsuccessful, but Caetano, aware of his lack of support, offered to resign. Then, in April 1974, the Carnation Revolution broke out. This conflict overthrew the government without any bloodshed or even resistance.

General António de Spínola did not take part in the bloodless military coup, but he benefited from it. He was inaugurated as president, and his new government made banks, large farms, and other industries the property of the state. There were strikes and a shortage of bread, and public transportation was in disarray. His government did not last, and over the next two years, six provisional governments came and went. Civil wars had erupted in the colonies that had suddenly been given independence, and this time Portuguese refugees fled back to their homeland.

In April 1975, 91 percent of all registered voters voted in an election that the Socialist Party of Dr. Mário Soares won with a slight majority. In due course, he was appointed prime minister. In 1987, Aníbal Cavaco Silva's Social Democrats were voted in with 50.15 percent of the votes. Soares had been elected president the year before and proved a highly popular nonparty leader who won reelection by a landslide in 1992. In 2005, the Socialist Party

Soldiers place carnations in their guns during the 1974 revolution.

won a huge victory, attaining its best election results in its history. From 2005 to 2011, the Socialist Party held onto power, with José Sócrates as prime minister. Following the Portuguese financial crisis, however, Sócrates resigned and the president dissolved parliament. The Social Democratic Party was voted into power in 2011 and Pedro Passos Coelho became Portugal's new prime minister.

Portugal joined the European Community in 1986 as its poorest member, in the hope that membership would ease its economic hardships. Billions of dollars of aid have subsequently been pumped into the Portuguese economy, and these were essentially used to restructure the country's business environment and rebuild infrastructure. When the global financial crisis came to a head in 2010, however, Portugal needed to ask for much more financial aid from the European Union in order to keep running its government and banks. For several years, this led to some political turmoil and allowed the Social Democratic Party to retake power.

INTERNET LINKS

news.bbc.co.uk/2/hi/europe/country_profiles/1101811.stm
Portugal's BBC timeline includes important dates from 1908 to 2012.

www.golisbon.com/culture/history.html
This site features a condensed but informative narrative of Portugal's history, complete with images and a list of historical sites.

www.nytimes.com/2007/07/23/world/europe/23iht-salazar.4.6790015.html?pagewanted=all
This *New York Times* article explains the conflicting opinions many in Portugal hold for António de Oliveira Salazar, the New State dictator.

www.visitportugal.com/en/content/historical-villages
Portugal's official tourism site includes a list of important historical villages.

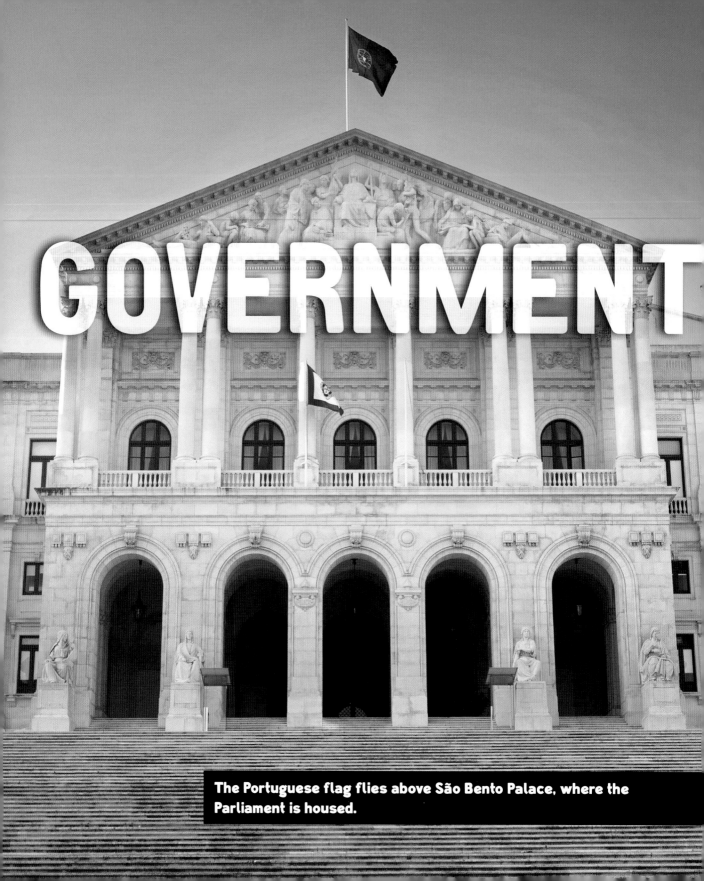

GOVERNMENT

The Portuguese flag flies above São Bento Palace, where the Parliament is housed.

3

OVER THE PAST TWO HUNDRED years, Portugal has been ruled by many kings and one queen, various elected parliaments, the military, and many dictators. During this period of time, the political needs of the Portuguese people were often ignored altogether in favor of the needs of a few powerful leaders. At first, it seemed as if the Carnation Revolution of 1974 would be just another military coup, but soon the military joined forces with regular Portuguese who wanted to create a system of government for themselves. With the passage of the Portuguese Constitution in 1976, a new form of government was set up: a democratic system governed by an elected parliament and a president (who, in turn, appoints the prime minister). The Portuguese fought for and finally achieved the democracy and, thus, the freedom that they enjoy today.

"Who is not patriotic cannot be considered Portuguese."
–António de Oliveira Salazar in 1975

PORTUGAL'S CONSTITUTIONS

Dom Pedro and his daughter, Maria, hold the Portuguese Constitution of 1826.

Since the 1820s, Portugal has had a number of constitutions; those of 1911 and 1976 were the most democratic. Portugal's First Republic was established in October 1910.

During the next sixteen years, Portugal was ruled by no fewer than forty-five governments. Under the First Republic (1910—1926), new laws created a two-chamber parliament with a president, abolished noble titles, and changed the national coinage from the *real* (RAY-al), meaning "royal," to the *escudo* (ess-KOO-do), meaning "shield." The Second Republic (1926—1974), known in Portugal as the New State, was a republic in name only, as the country was governed by António de Oliveira Salazar and his group for most of that time.

It was the Third Republic that saw the creation of the constitution of April 2, 1976, a precursor of the present constitution, which was approved on August 12, 1982. This abolished the military Council of the Revolution and reduced the role of the president, who was now elected through universal suffrage to serve a maximum of two five-year terms. In the election of 1991, Dr. Mário Soares was elected for his second term as president. In 1996, he was succeeded by Jorge Sampaió.

The president is the commander in chief of the armed forces. He has a council of state to advise him on the exercise of his discretionary powers. The council of state consists of senior officers and members selected by the president and the parliament. The president appoints a prime minister and a council of ministers. The prime minister is the head of the council of ministers.

The parliament, called the Assembly of the Republic, consists of 230 members (reduced from 250 in 1991) who are elected through universal suffrage to serve a four-year term. In 1989, the parliament approved further

MACAU

The Macau Peninsula at the mouth of the Pearl River in China was once governed as a Portuguese colony. It was first assumed by Portugal in 1557. Then, over the centuries, governance began to change. Eventually, based on an agreement made with the Chinese government in the 1980s, Macau became a Chinese territory under Portuguese governance and had administrative and economic autonomy. In 1999, it was finally completely handed over to China.

Today, tourism is a major industry there. Constant ferry-loads of visitors come from Hong Kong on the opposite bank each year. Many of them come for round-the-clock gambling at the many casinos in this "Las Vegas of the East." For centuries, people have visited the ancient Temple of the Goddess A-Ma, the patron goddess of fishermen.

The former Portuguese colonial headquarters in Macau.

Macau consists of the picturesque old city of Santa Nome de Deus de Macau, with its modern skyscraper waterfront, and the islands of Taipa and Colôane linked to the mainland by causeways. Most residents of Macau speak the local Cantonese dialect today as they did during the colonial period, even though the official language then was Portuguese.

reforms that spurred Portugal's gradual transition from a socialist economy to a more democratic and liberal one.

It is noteworthy that the 1974 revolution that brought years of dictatorship to an end came from the south of Portugal, where rich landowners wanted their share of running the country, whereas the changes introduced in the 1980s came from the north, where more conservative-minded owners of small properties were wary of change. Today, the only remains of the Portuguese empire are the autonomous regions of the Azores and Madeira. Both these groups of islands have their own locally elected governments, but their general laws fall under Portugal's constitution.

Pedro Passos Coelho served as prime minister of Portugal from 2011 to 2015.

PARLIAMENT

Historically, there have been four principal political parties in Portugal: Socialists, Social Democrats, Communists, and Christian Democrats. However, recent economic and political upheavals in the country have led these parties to form two major alliances: Portugal Ahead, a center-right alliance between the Social Democratic Party and the Christian Democrats, and the United Democratic Coalition, an alliance between the Portuguese Communist Party and the Ecologist Party. In most elections in recent years, the Social Democratic Party has held onto the majority of seats. The reverse happened in 2005, when the Socialists obtained their largest victory ever and secured the majority of the vote. The current prime minister of Portugal is Pedro Passos Coelho.

Legislative elections were held in 2015, during which Portugal Ahead won a clear majority of seats. The newly formed alliance won 36.8 percent of the vote and the Socialist Party came in second at 35 percent. Based on these elections, the parties currently represented in the parliament are Portugal Ahead (132 seats), the Socialist Party (74 seats), the United Democratic Coalition (16 seats), and the Left Bloc (8 seats). Voter turnout in the 2015 elections was the lowest ever at 57 percent. The presidential election will be held in 2016.

The parliament consists of 230 members, elected by twenty constituencies on a system of proportional representation. Every Portuguese citizen aged eighteen or older is entitled to vote.

MILITARY

Portugal is defended by armed forces made up of around thirty-three thousand active members. Half of the defense force used to be drafted through a program of compulsory military service that lasted four to eight months for the army, and four to eighteen months for the navy and air force. Those with valid reasons for avoiding military service were allowed to perform an alternative community service. Compulsory military service was abolished in 2004. Now Portuguese men aged eighteen and above can volunteer to join the military service.

The defense budget, like the armed forces of Portugal, is relatively small. In 2014, total military expenditure equaled about $2.5 billion, which was equivalent to about 1 percent of Portugal's gross domestic product (GDP).

The military consists of the army, navy, and air force. The army consists of conventional troops, plus the paramilitary National Republican Guard, Public Security Police, and Border Guard. The navy is divided into three commands: Lisbon and Portimão (for the mainland coastline), the Azores, and Madeira. Its most publicized activity is sea rescue. Lisbon served as the naval base of the North Atlantic Treaty Organization (NATO) Iberian Atlantic Command from 2004 until 2012. The air force is equipped with combat, training, and transportation aircraft.

The Portuguese National Republican Guard.

FOREIGN ALLIES

Portugal, as well as Spain, joined the European Community (which would later become the European Union) on January 1, 1986, a move that has done much to help the country's economy. Despite centuries of distrust and rivalry, Portugal and Spain decided to be allies and abolished most border controls. Since then, trade, investment, and tourism between the two countries have increased. Together, the two Iberian nations now have a stronger voice in European politics than either of them would have alone. Between 1992 and 2007, Portugal has served three times as president of the Council of the EU, most recently from July to December 2007.

Portugal is also a member of the United Nations (UN), NATO, and the Council of Europe. Meanwhile, strong cultural ties are maintained with other Portuguese-speaking countries, such as Angola, the Cape Verde Islands, East Timor, Guinea-Bissau, Mozambique, and São Tomé and Principe. Drawing on its strong historical ties, Portugal also tries to maintain a close relationship with Brazil.

Portugal's oldest ally is Britain. The Treaty of Windsor in 1386 declared perpetual peace and friendship. This agreement was followed a few centuries later by the Methuen Treaty of 1703. Hence, the longest-standing alliance of modern times was established. Among the terms of the more recent treaty is the provision that Portuguese wines will be admitted to Britain at a third less duty than that payable on French wines in perpetuity.

During World War I, Portugal answered Britain's request for assistance by seizing German ships sheltered in its ports. Then, in World War II, the Portuguese government gave Britain permission to build military bases on the Azores from which to attack German submarines in the Atlantic. During the Falklands War (1982), the British were once again allowed to use the Azores as a base for their naval operations.

Portugal held the presidency of the Council of the European Union in 2007.

NEW ADMINISTRATIVE DIVISIONS

Mainland Portugal was once divided into eighteen administrative districts (plus three in the Azores and one in Madeira), each with its own elected civil governor. While these districts were used for so long that they still hold importance to the Portuguese, they were made obsolete when different administrative regions were defined in 2013. The two new administrative divisions are metropolitan areas (divided into Lisbon and Porto regions) and inter-municipal communities. There are currently twenty-one inter-municipal communities in Portugal. Local administration is handled by municipal authorities in the towns and by parish assemblies in the villages.

The courts of justice are headed by the Constitutional Court and the Supreme Court of Justice in Lisbon. Under these are other judicial, administrative, tax, and military courts. They are divided into four judicial districts: Lisbon, Porto, Coimbra, and Évora. Each district has four courts of appeal. A tribunal checks new laws to ensure they agree with the terms of the constitution. As early as 1867, the death penalty for civil crimes was abolished.

The police forms three bodies: the Public Security Police, which maintains general public order and looks after city traffic; the National Republican Guard, which supplies armed police in rural areas and is responsible for highway patrol countrywide; and the Judicial Police, which investigates criminal cases.

Pickpockets do exist where there are large crowds, especially on the busy Lisbon subway. Theft is rampant, and the disturbing increase in crime is exacerbated by increasing poverty in urban areas where residents struggle to survive.

"The People are no longer afraid." –Cover of a Portuguese newspaper on May 12, 1974

INTERNET LINKS

www.angloportuguesesociety.org.uk/alliance-history
This in-depth article explains the long history of the Anglo-Portuguese alliance.

countrystudies.us/portugal/85.htm
You can learn more about the autonomous regions of Portugal, as well as Macau's history as a Portuguese colony, here.

app.parlamento.pt/site_antigo/ingles/cons_leg/Constitution_VII_revisao_definitive.pdf
This is the 2005 revision of the Constitution of the Portuguese Republic in English.

www.portugal.gov.pt/en.aspx
Learn about the newest election results and laws on the English version of the official Portuguese government website.

ECONOMY

These sloping vineyards play an important role in Portugal's economy.

4

PORTUGAL IS CLASSIFIED AS A high-income country, which means that the Portuguese enjoy a reasonably high standard of living. However, when Portugal entered into the European Union in 1986, it was Europe's poorest country.

Entering the Eurozone—or choosing along with many other countries in Europe to adopt a common currency and agree on issues as a region—brought some measure of economic stability to Portugal. During this time, farming began to play less of a role in the Portuguese economy, while financial services, hospitality, retail, technology, and other domains played a larger role. The European Union has provided the country with many benefits, such as funding for infrastructure, more roads and buildings, and improved trade ties. In 2002, Portugal replaced the escudo with the euro as its official currency.

While the Portuguese economy experienced above-average growth throughout most of the 1990s, it began to slow in the early 2000s. Then the global financial crisis of 2008 hit. Unemployment rates increased rapidly, and the Portuguese government began going further into debt. By 2010, two large Portuguese banks failed, which means that they could no longer cover their expenses. This was a very stressful time for Portugal and for the EU—if a large economy like Portugal's could go into crisis, no other countries were safe.

In 2011, the European Union and the International Monetary Fund provided a financial bailout worth €78 billion ($111 billion) to Portugal, following similar financial aid to Greece and the Republic of Ireland. This meant that Portugal would receive the money it needed to keep

The Strategic Plan for Transport in Portugal for 2011-2015 includes a plan to: "rationalize networks and improve mobility and logistic conditions in Portugal; improve energy efficiency and reduce environmental impact; (and) reduce transport costs and ensure financial sustainability of the companies …" –From the International Monetary Fund's 2012 Report on Portugal

running, but it would have to follow certain regulations and eventually repay its debt. After this bailout, the Portuguese economy stabilized, and in 2014, the country announced that it had returned to previous economic levels.

This doesn't mean that Portugal's economic challenges are over, however. Some economists think that Portugal's economic recovery is not sustainable and that it could face more challenges ahead. Where Portugal's economy will go from here remains to be seen.

AGRICULTURE

Portugal is a land of fruit, wine, and trees. For centuries, more than half of Portugal's population was engaged in some form of agriculture. Grapes, olives, oats, wheat, barley, corn, rice, apples, pears, oranges, peaches, and tomatoes are still grown for domestic use and for export. Portugal is one of the world's most established wine producers. Its varied geographic terrain allows for the growth of different varieties of grapes. Its most famous vineyards are located in the Douro River Valley and in the Minho, where exceptional table wines and rich, red port wine are produced.

Portugal is the world's fourth-largest exporter of processed tomatoes. Today, however, only 10 percent of the workforce is engaged in agriculture. For many years, agriculture lost thousands of workers to the manufacturing and service sectors, which employ 25 and 65 percent of the workforce, respectively. However, following the financial crisis of 2010, many Portuguese began to leave large, expensive cities and their jobs in service and industry to return to the land, in part due to governmental programs to encourage farming. In 2013 alone, the number of farming jobs rose 10.6 percent, which was the largest increase in all sectors of the Portuguese economy.

As many young people are returning to farming to support themselves, the cultivation and production of cork remains an important part of the economy. Half of the world's cork—54 percent, or 185,000 tons (167,829 metric tons), in 2002—comes from 1,680,317 acres (680,000 hectares) of cork forests in Portugal's Alentejo and Algarve regions.

Besides being made into wine bottle stoppers, the cork is used for insulation, fishing floats, tiles, and such sporting essentials as ping-pong paddles and badminton shuttlecocks. The cork trade generates more than €800 million ($900 million) a year in export revenues. Although profitable, it is a slow moneymaker. According to the law, cork bark may only be stripped from a tree once every nine years.

BUSINESS AND INDUSTRY

Portugal is rapidly industrializing. Industries used to be state-owned, but in the 1990s and the beginning of the twenty-first century, increasing privatization occurred in many key sectors, such as highways, telecommunications, oil, tobacco, electrical utilities, and cement. Portugal produces textiles and clothing—constituting nearly a third of all exports—as well as canned sardines, tuna, tomato concentrate, ceramics, paper pulp, fertilizers, and refined olive oil. There are two large shipbuilding and repair yards located in Lisbon and Setúbal, as well as a modern steelworks.

Angry protestors clash with police during demonstrations against the actions of Portuguese banks.

The now closed Lousal Mine was once an important pyrite mine in Portugal.

Portugal has limited resources in the production of energy. Among the European countries, it still registers the lowest per capita power production. Its largest domestic energy source is hydroelectric power, which is highly dependent on the amount of rain the region receives. Most of the energy consumed by Portugal is derived from crude oil, which is imported from other countries. Coal is no longer produced for export since Portugal's last coal mine closed in 1994. Coal, however, provides for 23 percent of energy consumption. Natural gas was introduced in Portugal in 1997, and consumption of this energy source, which is imported from Algeria and Spain, has been increasing. Natural gas provided for 18 percent of energy consumption in 2012. In recent years, the Portuguese government has been moving toward energy diversification and developing renewable and sustainable energy sources. In 2004, a budget of $51.4 million was set aside for twenty wind energy projects. Since then, many more wind farms have been inaugurated, including, the Alto Minho Wind Farm in 2008, which was Europe's largest on-shore wind farm at the time of its completion.

Although there are no sources of oil or gas in Portugal, the country has several significant mineral resources. Iron and tin deposits are worked in the north, as well as wolframite, a hard mineral used in making tungsten for electrical equipment. There are large reserves of copper and uranium, and a little gold. Limestone, granite, and good quality marble are quarried for local construction.

FISHING INDUSTRY

The Portuguese fishing industry is large with many subsectors. In addition to the fishermen who go out to sea in fishing vessels, there are canning and drying industries that prepare the fish for export. The fishing industry also

The oldest bookstore in the world is tucked away in the historic Chiado neighborhood of Lisbon, nestled between a coffee shop and the Opera. The Bertrand Bookstore first opened in 1732, although it had to change addresses (however, it remained on the same street—Rua Garrett) in 1755, when the original building was destroyed in the great Lisbon earthquake.

The popular bookstore is covered with original wood paneling and is very popular with tourists. In 2015, the store completed renovations. It now has a coffee shop and a dedicated room for cultural events. The bookstore is so influential that it has its own font named after it, and the Bertrand Group, which owns the bookstore, also owns fifty-three bookstores and eight publishing houses across Portugal. All of Portugal's most famous and well-loved writers are represented on its bookshelves, including Fernando Pessoa and José Saramago.

employs researchers to study fishing techniques and develop aquaculture. Large organizations and traditional subsistence fishermen are all part of this diverse industry.

Sardines, cod, tuna, and some lobster and shellfish make up the bulk of the catch. The wooden-hulled boats with high, broad bows, called *traineiras* (tray-NEY-ras), are painted bright colors. This enables fishermen to recognize individual boats from a distance.

Loans from the EU have benefited the Portuguese fishing industry by providing better boats and equipment. Fishing provided work for over eighteen thousand people in 2009. However, Portugal still cannot supply enough fish to meet local needs. The fishing industry, therefore, has more challenges to tackle, such as diminishing catches, an aging workforce, structural problems, and poor working conditions.

A traditional *traineira* sails the translucent blue waters off Portugal.

TOURISM AND HOSPITALITY

Portugal is a haven for tourists. A beautiful coastline and a verdant, tranquil landscape have made Portugal a popular tourist destination. Some eight million tourists bring in about $16 billion in foreign revenue each year. Lisbon is a popular European city for travelers, along with the beaches of the Algarve. The rugged hills of the Trás-os-Montes, with their natural forests and terraced vineyards, are a popular tourist attraction, too.

Portugal has been quick to realize the possibilities of attracting tourists. In addition to 1,700 hotels around the country, it has converted many historic palaces, convents, and castles into *pousadas* where visitors can sample hospitality of a more traditional and gracious style. There are also youth hostels, camping parks, and simple accommodations offered in farms and private houses.

IMPORTS AND EXPORTS

Trade has been in Portuguese blood for many centuries. As the country's sailors discovered fresh lands in Africa, its traders arrived with food crops, fine horses, and sharp weapons from different parts of the world. In exchange, they took away gold, ivory, and slaves.

Today, most trading is done with EU members. Border controls with Spain and some other countries have been abolished. Nearly half of Portugal's food is imported from fellow European countries. The major imports are machinery and transportation equipment, chemicals, petroleum, textiles, and agricultural products. Major exports include clothing and footwear, machinery, chemicals, cork, paper products, and hides.

Portugal imports more than it exports; and the higher wages negotiated by the country's strong trade unions have increased production costs, rendering Portuguese products less competitive in the international marketplace.

Outside of Europe, Portugal is building strong financial contacts with the United States and Japan. Trade with Japan began as early as 1543, when firearms were introduced to that country in exchange for silver. Now Japanese investment is welcomed in Portugal.

THE WORKFORCE

In 2004, the unemployment rate in Portugal was lower than elsewhere in Europe, at only 6.5 percent. However, after the financial crisis, unemployment rose to a record of 17.7 percent in 2013. This number has been gradually decreasing since then, and it settled at 11.9 percent by 2015. Many economists are hopeful that the unemployment rate will continue to drop. While Portugal has social security benefits for employees, it also has one of the lowest average income rates for workers among countries in the EU. These low wages, combined with the high unemployment rate, have enticed many young people to leave Portugal and seek work elsewhere.

Labor unions are active in Portugal. Trade unions, employers, and the government have a commitment to peaceful negotiations and are working toward improvements in working conditions.

During the dictatorship (1926—1974), workers were forbidden to strike, but all that changed with the 1974 revolution. Legal trade unions initiated a constant wave of strikes for fairer employment practices. Today, there are two large trade unions for workers: the Workers' General Union (UGT) and the General Confederation of Portuguese Workers (CGTP).

Portugal's per capita income has risen slightly from around $25,990 in 2010 to $26,170, in 2013. While per capita income has not increased much since the financial crisis, it is still much higher than its per capita income of $11,170 in 1990. The country remains one of the poorest nations in Europe. The government is working to upgrade agriculture, industry, and public services, such as the telephone and transportation systems, all of which have traditionally needed many workers.

The popular Japanese sweet Konpeito is named after the Portuguese word for candy.

TRANSPORT

Officially, Portugal has 10,650 miles (17,135 km) of paved and unpaved roads, and 1,771 miles (2,850 km) of railways. An expressway has been completed between Lisbon and Porto.

Driving in Portugal is a dangerous adventure. The number of deaths caused by road accidents in Portugal is higher than the European average. Many agree that this can be attributed to a combination of bad roads with unreliable signage and reckless drivers. Many prefer to travel by the economical train service despite the long lines for tickets. A few express trains, called *rápidos* (RAP-ee-dos), provide fast luxury travel between major towns.

A labor demonstration held in Guimarães in 2007.

Once a proud sailing nation, Portugal no longer has a great fleet, although Lisbon and Porto remain busy commercial ports. Portline is a company that operates commercial transportation, mostly between Portugal and northern Europe or Portuguese-speaking countries in Africa. There are international airports in Lisbon, Porto, and Faro (in the Algarve) and in the Azores and Madeira.

WHERE TO GO FROM HERE

Since Portugal's admission into the EU, restructuring of the economy through policy changes and increasing privatization has created immense opportunities for the Portuguese. Portugal made the euro its official currency in 2002. Following the major setback of the financial crisis, Portugal's economy seems to be regaining strength. With help from the EU's three-year aid package, major financial reforms, and a change in government, Portugal's economy has expanded since 2013, its unemployment rate has dropped, and its deficit has been reduced. However, many experts continue to be cautious about the future of Portugal's economy. If the Portuguese recovery can be sustained, this would be a good sign for the continued health of the European and global financial markets. If Portugal's economy encounters any more trouble, this could be a sign of worse things to come.

This Lisbon mural reads, in part: "The power lies in the people."

INTERNET LINKS

www.businessinsider.com/portuguese-people-are-returning-to-farming-in-droves-2012-4
This Reuters article explains how young Portuguese people turned back to agriculture in the absence of available corporate jobs during the economic downturn.

www.dw.com/en/lisbon-home-to-worlds-oldest-bookstore/a-18142887
This article describes Bertrand Bookstore's long history and recent renovations.

ec.europa.eu/economy_finance/publications/occasional_paper/2011/op79_en.htm
This European Commission report describes the bailout program for Portugal.

theportugueseeconomy.blogspot.com
This blog is dedicated to the state of Portugal's economy.

ENVIRONMENT

Wind farms produce renewable energy near Farfe, Portugal.

5

PORTUGAL IS A BREATHTAKINGLY beautiful country with an incredible range of terrain and weather conditions. The mountain ranges of the north teem with natural life, while the rolling plains of the Algarve and Alentejo are filled with farms that provide locals with important crops to eat. Portugal's coast is famous for its beaches, cliffs, and coves, and its waters are filled with a rich variety of marine life that provides the ingredients for Portugal's famous seafood. But these important natural resources can only continue if they are protected from overexploitation.

The Portuguese Environment Agency was created in 2012. It aims to protect the Portuguese ecosystem, improve knowledge about environmental conservation, and increase public participation in environmental activities. As of 2015, it works within the Portuguese Ministry of the Environment, Territory Management and Energy, and employs eight hundred highly skilled employees and consultants. Despite the recent economic crises, Portugal is committed to developing environmental sustainability, especially through its use of energy.

"The relationship between the economy and the environment is, at the moment, particularly relevant. Portugal is strongly committed to simultaneously improving economic growth, job creation, and environmental conditions."
–European Environment Agency

REDUCING AIR POLLUTION

Portugal has signed numerous international environmental agreements and protocols aimed at protecting and sustaining the environment as well as conserving Earth's biodiversity. It was the sixteenth country to ratify the Protocol to Abate Acidification, Eutrophication, and Ground-level Ozone in 2005.

Yet despite Portugal's high-profile participation in these international agreements and its seemingly active advocacy for the environment, it was among eight EU countries taken to court by the European Commission—an institution that upholds the interests of the EU as a whole—in 2002 for failing to take proper measures to fight air pollution that year.

The European Commission report states that Portugal had the biggest increase (32 percent) in greenhouse gas emissions among EU member states between 1990 and 1998. During that period of time, it was also the country with the second-largest increase (25 percent) in carbon dioxide emissions, exceeding the desired limits set in the Kyoto Protocol. However, due to Portugal's efforts, it has been one of the few European countries with declining greenhouse gas emissions from 2009 and 2010. In fact, since 2009, emissions have decreased steadily in Portugal. The country continues to be on track to remain below the limits set by the Kyoto agreement.

Air pollution continues to be one of Portugal's most crucial environmental problems. Portugal has tried to comply with EU standards whenever possible. In an attempt to promote the use of public transportation and to raise awareness of the harmful effects of motor vehicle emissions, a car-free day was implemented in 2000 in the city of Porto. No motor vehicles were allowed on the road that day. This practice has continued, and as of 2015, fifty-seven Portuguese cities and towns have taken part in World Car-Free Day, which is held every year on September 22. However, more needs to be done for Portugal to reduce its air pollution levels on a more permanent basis.

Forest fires are also another source of air pollution. The summers of 2003 and 2004 were among the hottest in five hundred years. They also saw the worst forest fires in Portugal. The fires had a devastating effect on the Portuguese economy and environment. They wiped out large areas of valuable woodland—as extensive as 531,277 acres (215,000 ha)—and led to massive soil erosion. As a result, water bodies such as rivers and lakes were polluted by silt and chemical run-off. The fires claimed more than eighteen lives, and people lost their homes and farms. The cleanup efforts cost the government €1 billion ($1.1 billion), and foreign aid was necessary to help in the reconstruction process.

While there was some improvement in the years after 2005, as of 2015, forest fires may once again cause great damage in Portugal. The region is experiencing one of the worst droughts since records began seventy years ago. With high temperatures and a lack of rain, the risk of large forest fires across the Iberian Peninsula greatly increases.

NATIONAL PARKS AND PROTECTED AREAS

Portugal has one national park, thirteen natural parks, nine natural reserves, seven natural monuments, and two protected landscapes. While there are many areas set aside specifically for conservation, they do not stand in the way of the development of renewable energy resources.

Nevertheless, there is a sizable amount of land classified as protected areas. One of these is Parque Nacional da Peneda-Gerês, situated in the Minho. Created in 1971, it is Portugal's only national park and the first park to be set aside for conservation. It covers 177,916 acres (72,000 ha) and has great historical and environmental significance. It is home to the wolf, the royal eagle, and 147 other Portuguese birds, such as the honey buzzard and the whinchat. The park has a variety of climates, and as a result, rare flora and fauna can be found there. The park was also set up to preserve its human inhabitants' traditional ways of living. Archaeological remains, ancient shrines, and monasteries can be found within the park's grounds. There are also pre-Roman Celtic villages (called *castros*), in addition to a few Portuguese farming villages, in the intriguing park. These traditional Portuguese villages are fast diminishing in number because the lure of the city has proven too great for the young to resist. A reported nine thousand people live within the park, and it is not unusual for three-quarters of the inhabitants within a single village to be elderly.

The picturesque Peneda-Gerês National Park.

The Parque Natural da Serra da Estrela was established in 1976. This park is located in the highest mountains of Portugal, the Serra da Estrela, on a high plateau crossed by the Rio Mondego and Rio Zêzere valleys. The park spans 386 square miles (1000 sq km) and about half of its area is at an altitude of 2,297 feet (700 m). The area features terrain that was shaped by glacial ice, including ravines, valley structures, and rocks left behind in the complex landscape. Here, one can find the wall lizard, a unique inhabitant of the region. Other fauna include otters, genets, badgers, wild cats, water moles, red-breasted bullfinches, and midwife frogs.

In addition, ancient Roman, Arab, and Visigothic architectural remains can still be found in Parque Natural da Serra da Estrela. There are three main walking trails that take three to four days to complete. On a clear day, the sea can be seen from about 93 miles (150 km) away.

LARGE DAM PROGRAM

One of the most unpopular and contentious economic strategies that the Portuguese government has adopted is the building of large dams. Dams that are more than 49.2 feet (15 m) in height and hold a reservoir volume of more than 792.5 million gallons (3 million cubic meters) are classified as large dams. As of 2015, there are about 217 large dams in Portugal. Hydroelectric power accounts for 37 percent of the country's total energy consumption.

In the late twentieth century, the government, ironically funded by the European Commission, began the construction of the Alqueva Dam in the Alentejo region. The construction led to a large number of protests from nongovernmental organizations and international conservation agencies, such as the World Wildlife Fund and Friends of the Earth, who formed a coalition to oppose the construction of the dam.

The building of the dam was the largest deforestation program in Europe, resulting in a tremendous loss of precious biodiversity. In addition to this, the dam was to be built between two seismic fault lines. Disastrous floods could result from mudslides or an earthquake. The severity of the possible environmental fallout should therefore not be underestimated.

Yet despite all the international disapproval, construction of the dam continued and it was completed in 2002 at the cost of $1.7 billion. It is the biggest dam in Europe. Its environmental and ecological costs reached a massive scale, and eagles, kites, wild boars, and the Iberian lynx were among the species that were endangered.

The controversial Alqueva Dam in the Alentejo.

The Portuguese government is in the final stages of building a new dam across the Sabor River in northeastern Portugal (Trás-os-Montes). Following the start of the project in 2008, plans for the Baixo Sabor Dam have led to a huge uproar in both environmental and scientific circles. There has been a prevalent fear that the building of the dam will destroy the habitat of endangered animals and birds such as the golden eagle, Egyptian vulture, Bonelli's eagle, and black stork, and also result in the displacement of the resident agrarian population, leading to an eventual irreversible loss of their rich heritage, ancient traditions, and festivals. The loss of this agrarian culture would truly be a great loss for the Portuguese.

There are other reasons why many believe the dam should not be built. First, dams in the north have not proven their worth to economic development. There has been little progress in the local communities served by the large number of dams along the rivers, and the residents remain the poorest people in the country. Second, the many small but viable olive farms along the valley will be adversely affected by the dam. Should floodwaters rise, these farmers will lose their livelihood. Flooding the valley destroys not just the trees but a significant source of revenue for the country, too, as the valley produces some 15,850 gallons (60,000 liters) of olive oil for Portugal.

Portugal is a perfect country for solar power plants because it has many days of sun every year. By the end of 2013, solar power supplied energy to 166,500 Portuguese homes, an increase of 25 percent from the previous year. Part of the reason for this increase is the government's focus on building large solar power plants across the country. The largest of these—the largest solar power plant ever built at the time of its construction in 2008—is the Moura Photovoltaic Power Station in Amareleja, Portugal.

The Moura Power Station comprises 376,000 solar panels spread out over 618 acres (250 ha) of land. Construction was completed in 2010. In order to supply the solar panels for the power plant, a solar panel factory was built nearby. It is now producing solar panels for international buyers as well. In total, the Moura Power Station can produce 45 megawatts (MW) of electricity each year, which is enough to power thirty thousand homes!

Nonetheless, the government sees the Baixo Sabor Dam as a reliable source of hydroelectric power and renewable energy. This is based on its belief that the alternative energy produced by the dam will help reduce greenhouse gases and fight climate change. However, reports reveal that the projected energy produced will provide only 0.6 percent of the energy consumed in Portugal. Any benefit to the climate will be relatively insignificant, considering the harm the dam will bring to the ecosystem.

THE PROBLEM OF SOIL EROSION

One of the causes of soil erosion is the poor management of irrigation systems, leading to substantial soil runoff. The forest fires of 2003 and 2004 also created conditions for soil erosion.

The environmental situation in Portugal, as in any country, is complex. Sometimes measures taken to work toward sustainability seem to contradict one another. For example, even while action is taken to clean the Douro River, protesters object to the building of a waste treatment plant that would pollute another river.

Environmental problems also spread across the boundaries of countries. Portugal suffers the effects of acid rain from clouds blown in from other European countries. And while it is true that Portugal is one of the largest producers of greenhouse gases in Europe, other countries may also own the factories that contribute to the high emissions. Portugal was recently taken to task for promoting illegal logging in Brazil. Portuguese ports have reportedly been the means by which illegal loggers enter the European market.

Nevertheless, it is hoped that Portugal's involvement in multilateral conservation efforts with fellow EU members, its commitment to the environmental policies initiated by the European Union, and its participation in international environmental agreements will help the country in its efforts to contain and resolve the environmental challenges it now faces.

Evidence of coastal erosion in Albufeira.

INTERNET LINKS

www.acciona.com/business-divisions/energy/emblematic-projects/amareleja-photovoltaic-pv-solar-plant
You can read more about Acciona, the company that built the Moura Power Plant, on their official website.

travel.nationalgeographic.com/travel/parks/peneda-geres-portugal
This is a National Geographic guide to Peneda-Gerês National Park.

www.portugaltravelguide.com/index.php/top-pot-pourri/202-seven-natural-wonders
This is a brief article describing the seven natural wonders of Portugal, according to 656,000 voters who took part in an online poll in 2015.

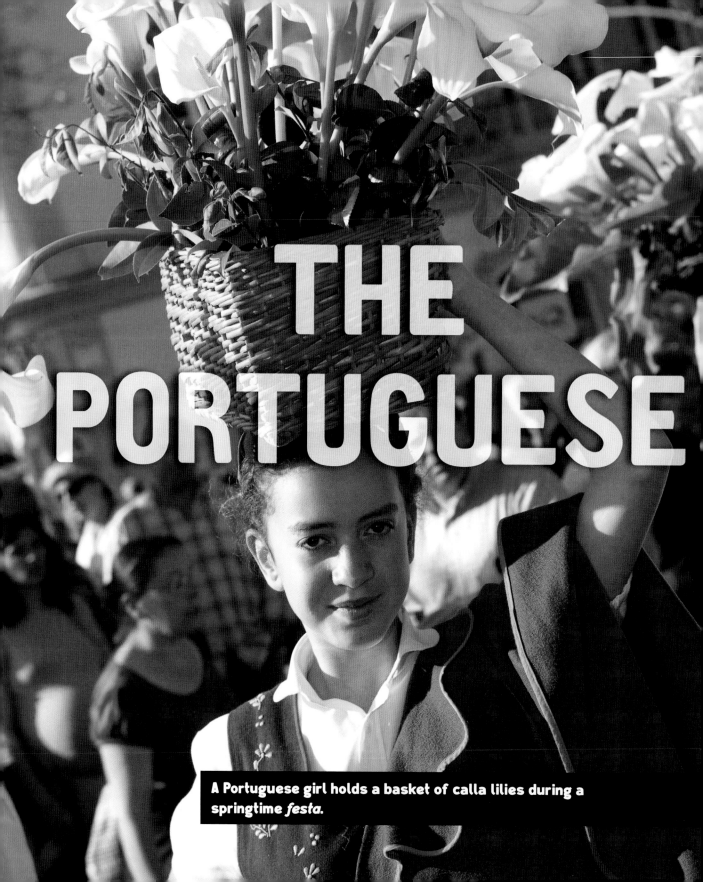

THE PORTUGUESE

A Portuguese girl holds a basket of calla lilies during a springtime *festa*.

6

THE PORTUGUESE HAIL FROM MANY different ethnic backgrounds and are proof of the country's rich history of cultural exchange. However, the Celts are often noted as an early group of people who populated prehistoric Portugal, and they contribute to the background of many Portuguese people today.

The Celts were various tribes with certain cultural similarities that spread across central and western Europe, including Britain and Ireland, during the Iron Age. They arrived on the Iberian Peninsula around 700 BCE, where they intermarried with the Iberians. The Citânia de Briteiros in Guimarães is an important ancient Celtic village and archaeological site in northern Portugal.

Celtic tribes entering the Iberian Peninsula must have come into contact with the Lusitanians, an indigenous group that lived between the Douro and Tagus Rivers. Some scholars hypothesize that the Luistanians gradually became dominated by the Celts—so much so that some scholars today are not quite sure whether the Luistanians were originally Celtic, too. The Lusitanians were the largest tribe in Portugal at the time, but they were by no means the only one. In fact, Portugal was peopled by many different tribes that lived together. Then, the Roman Empire entered the Iberian Peninsula and everything changed.

In 210 BCE, the Roman conquest of the Iberian Peninsula began. It lasted for over fifty years, with the Lusitanians fighting valiantly against their conquerors. In 150 BCE, the Romans conquered the Lusitanians;

"If we wish to locate Portuguese politeness … we could say that gregarious relationships, consensus and tact are favoured over confrontation, frankness or the protection of an individual's territory." –From "Politeness in Portugal" by Maria Helena Araújo Carreira

thousands were killed, and many more thousands were sold into slavery. Gradually, the tribes of Portugal were Romanized; in fact, Portuguese has evolved from the Romans' language, Latin.

By the fifth century CE, the Romans lost power to the successive invasions of Germanic tribes. The Suevi and the Vandals led the way, followed by the Visigoths, who subsequently conquered the entire Iberian Peninsula. The fair hair and blue eyes from these Germanic people can still be seen in the Portuguese people of the Minho and Trás-os-Montes regions.

In the eighth century, another important conquest took place: the Moors and the Arabs invaded the Iberian Peninsula from North Africa. They held onto power in Iberia until 1492, with the fall of Granada. Arab influence can still be seen in many important buildings in the south of Portugal, especially in Paderne Castle in the Algarve. Most Portuguese people today have the common Mediterranean characteristics of the Moors, with brown or black hair and brown eyes.

Today, the population of Portugal is 10.56 million. Many people have emigrated from Portugal to Brazil, Europe, or the United States to seek better conditions, especially after the recent financial crisis. However, 60 percent of the young people who left the country in 2011 have returned to start businesses and reinvigorate their cities and towns. The Portuguese are working hard to build a better future for themselves and for their children.

IDENTITY

Portuguese ways are a mixture of old and new. They cling to superstitious traditions yet are proud of the changes taking place around them. The warmth of the Mediterranean blends with the tough challenge of the Atlantic. In the midst of diversity, however, there seems to be a common characteristic: for all Portuguese, time is unimportant. No one is ever in a hurry.

The Portuguese are openly hospitable. They quarrel loudly, reconcile swiftly, and welcome visitors with great courtesy. Chatting, or bantering, is one of the national pleasures and takes place across the seats of a bus, out of the window to passersby, or while wobbling along on a bicycle over cobblestones. But to the Portuguese, surviving on the year's harvest, or celebrating in better times, is more important than the broader vision of the European Union. There is a general characteristic of *saudade* (sow-DAH-de), a melancholic and nostalgic feeling among the people, as if the past takes precedence over the future. However, this, too, is changing gradually as Portugal becomes involved in global dynamics and takes a strong and active role in the European community.

A woman sells daisies in Braga.

URBAN AND RURAL POPULATION

The population density is higher in the north than in the south (apart from the overpopulated Algarve coast) and more concentrated along the coast than inland. As with other countries worldwide, there is a steady trickle of urbanization. Young people eager to make their way in the world leave their rural upbringing in the hope of finding better jobs in the urban sprawls around Lisbon and Porto.

In a land of sunbaked plains, remote mountain villages, industrial harbors, and tourist-filled beaches, it is hardly surprising to find regional differences in the ways the Portuguese live. It is a land split apart by mountain ranges. Each discrete area has its own traditions.

In northern Trás-os-Montes, the village folk lead a simple and self-sufficient lifestyle, living a communal life that has not changed for centuries. In Monsanto, there are houses carved out of solid granite rock. Ox carts run on wooden wheels and oxen can be seen hauling a handheld plough. In the Minho, the harvest festival is a joyous celebration of songs, jubilant dances, drink, and much merry-making.

In the southern regions of the Algarve and Alentejo, the Moorish legacy is evident in the way they cherish water and trees. The Alentejanos appreciate a clean environment. Their old walled towns are litter-free.

JEWS IN PORTUGAL

Jewish families have lived in Portugal for over one thousand years. They first settled in the country around the eighth century, during the time of

Slavery was a major institution in Portugal from the time of the Romans, when they enslaved members of the conquered Celtic tribes. When Portuguese explorers reached the shores of Japan in 1543, they began to purchase Japanese men and women to sell as slaves in Portugal and around the world. Chinese slaves were also bought and sold by Portuguese traders. These men and women were treated horribly by slave traders and owners; they were often physically punished, tortured, branded, and separated from their families in the most horrific ways possible.

While the Portuguese participated in the slave trade, they also banned certain activities very early on compared to other European countries. In 1595, the Portuguese monarchy banned the buying and selling of Chinese slaves. This did not fully stop the Chinese slave trade, but it did reduce it drastically. The African slave trade continued for over 150 years, during which time the Portuguese brought many African slaves to American plantations. In 1761, the Marquis of Pombal banned all forms of slavery in mainland Portugal. Other European nations, such as Great Britain, only abolished slavery in the nineteenth century!

the Moors. In 1446, a royal ordinance decreed that the Jews had to live in segregated quarters called Judiaria. Compared to other European countries of the time, however, Portugal was considered a relatively safe place for Jews to live and work. In time, they came to wield considerable power as professionals such as doctors, financiers, astronomers, printers, and the world's finest mapmakers.

In 1492, in the course of religious persecution, Spain expelled its Jews and about sixty thousand fled to Portugal. They settled in Guarda, Belmonte, Tomar, Bragança, and Viana do Castelo. Four years later, however, the sanctuary offered to them in Portugal was repealed. In an attempt to retain their financial expertise at a time of burgeoning wealth, they were offered the option of being baptized as "New Christians." Many refused and were persecuted, seized, and burned, while others escaped to Morocco, Brazil, and the Netherlands, or to start the first Jewish community in New York. Others stayed on and continued to exercise their faith in secret as "Hidden Jews."

Today, small groups of Portuguese Jews remain, still clinging to their Jewish origins. Curiously, all their family names signify the names of plants, animals, or birds. Many Portuguese probably have some Jewish blood following centuries of intermarriage.

A SEAFARING PEOPLE

The sea has always been the greatest influence on the Portuguese as a people. Its shores have beckoned many and have made several true seafaring people. They are sturdily proud of such explorers as Bartolomeu Dias and Vasco da Gama. The Atlantic governs their weather and the fish harvest; the Mediterranean brings the tourists.

The interior of the Shaarei Tikva synagogue in Lisbon.

For years, some of the fishing boats would set sail from Lisbon for the Grand Banks off Newfoundland. They took dories (one-man fishing boats) in which fishermen went out alone to fish for cod. They then brought their catch back to the mother ship to be salted and stored. After six months, they returned to Portugal, where the fish were dried in the sun. Such old fishing styles have not totally died out.

The fishermen's boats, once launched over log rollers and pulled ashore by yoked oxen, may now have slipways and motorized hoists. However, that does not make fishing any less dangerous. Fishermen and their families tend to face the future a day at a time. A general fatalistic acceptance by sailors' families of the dangers of the sea is echoed in the sad singing of the *fadista* (fa-DIS-ta), or *fado* singer.

EMIGRANTS

With the blood of ancient explorers in their veins, the Portuguese have seldom hesitated to sail off to find fortune in some distant land. The first great gold rush was to Brazil. Whole families emigrated, crammed into packed boats. Between 1886 and 1926, over a million people left Portugal,

A Portuguese flag flies outside of the Portuguese embassy in Paris, France.

driven out by poverty and civil war at home. Another million left during the dictatorship of Salazar. It is estimated that there were five million Portuguese living abroad between 1965 and 1974. Some emigrated to the United States, about 50,000 to Australia, some 600,000 to South Africa, well over a million to Brazil, over two million to Europe, and 400,000 to Venezuela.

However, there were also the *retornados* (re-tor-NAH-dose), those who chose to return, like the 700,000 refugees from war-torn Angola and Mozambique. Some brought back skills and new ideas to challenge the old traditions at home, while others brought further poverty to a country that was already steeped in it. Over 100,000 returned in 1990, including 45,000 from Africa, 11,000 from Brazil, 8,000 from the United Kingdom, and 7,000 from the United States.

Following the financial crisis of 2011, approximately 485,000 people, many of them young university graduates, left Portugal in search of better opportunities. Of these, 60 percent have become retornados. Many traveled north to France, where it is said that Paris has the largest Portuguese population of any city after Lisbon. Others left Portugal for the United States, Britain, Switzerland, or to the many Portuguese-speaking countries around the world.

TRADITIONAL ATTIRE

The closest thing to a Portuguese national costume is still worn in the Minho. The women wear a loose white blouse with a finely worked, lace-trimmed neckline and cuffs, a full skirt with several petticoats, and a scarf around the neck or head. In chillier weather, a black shawl is added.

Some Portuguese women continue to wear the traditional black of mourning. By tradition, black should be worn for two years in memory of a dead father, and one year for any other relative. A widow wears black for the rest of her life.

For men, the traditional attire consists of a white, collarless shirt, perhaps with a black jacket or decorated vest; black pants; and a wide-brimmed, flat-topped black hat. Alentejo cattlemen still wear their traditional red and green stocking caps, and the women often sport a black trilby hat to go with colorful floral skirts. Traditional costumes are worn during festivals, too.

In tourist centers such as Nazaré, the fishermen wear bright plaid shirts, checkered pants, and tasseled woolen stocking caps, making more money posing for photographs than actually fishing. The women sport elaborately tied headscarves and crocheted petticoats.

This couple wears traditional Portuguese costumes during an accordion performance.

INTERNET LINKS

www.jewishvirtuallibrary.org/jsource/vjw/Portugal.html
This page on the Jewish Virtual Library website examines the history of Jews in Portugal.

ldhi.library.cofc.edu/exhibits/show/african_laborers_for_a_new_emp/launching_the_portuguese_slave
The Lowcounty Digital History Initiative gives the history of the slave trade in Portugal from the 1400s to its abolition.

www.thelovelyplanet.net/traditional-dress-of-portugal-a-gift-of-centuries-old-civilization
This site has lots of great pictures of traditional Portuguese clothing.

www.npr.org/sections/altlatino/2014/02/28/282552613/saudade-an-untranslatable-undeniably-potent-word
Listen to the audio broadcast on NPR explaining the meaning of saudade.

LIFESTYLE

Enjoying the social aspect of meals is an important part of Portuguese culture.

7

PORTUGUESE LIFE REVOLVES AROUND the family. This is due to cultural, religious, and even political reasons. Under Salazar's Estado Novo (New State), state organization was based on the family unit. Only men who were heads of households were allowed to vote and wives were subject to their husbands' authority; marriage was permanent because divorce was unknown. After the Carnation Revolution, this began to change gradually. Today, many Portuguese women work outside of the home and the rate of marriage is declining.

Despite increasing modernization, Portugal's culture and lifestyle is still deeply rooted in tradition, and especially Catholic tradition. Life in the bustling cities may be like life in any globalized city around the world, but life in the Portuguese countryside is slower to change. This is especially true in the north, which has resisted centuries of conquest by outsiders and is more isolated in its ways. Southerners tend to be more open to change.

Today, many foreigners are enticed with Portugal's slower lifestyle. The Portuguese still live at a Mediterranean pace, which means that

"In the same way as (the Italian dictator) Mussolini, Salazar only considered women in terms of their role as mothers and never as women, citizens or workers." -Madelena Barbosa in "Women in Portugal"

they can often be late, take longer breaks and vacations, and often care more about appreciating the good things in life than worrying about getting everything done. This, however, is changing rapidly in big cities, where there is pressure to keep pace with large and efficient foreign economies. Time will tell how Portugal's economic problems will influence the structure and pace of Portuguese life as well.

FAMILY LIFE

The mother is the accepted head of the family. In the outside world of politics and power, the voices of women are increasingly being considered seriously, but in the family the mother has the final say.

Large families still exist in the country. Traditionally, young people live at home until they marry; then their grandparents can help babysit. The desire to remain together as an extended family is easy to understand because so many families live on their own small farms. However, as the family grows, overcrowding results, leading to emigration from the rural areas.

A young boy and girl dress in traditional attire during the Festival of the Roses.

CHANGING BELIEFS

Globalization is bringing change to Portugal, though more in the swelling towns than in the conservative countryside. Statistics reveal that marriage rates are declining rapidly. The divorce rate is increasing, particularly among city dwellers. The Roman Catholic Church remains opposed to contraception and abortion, although abortion was legalized in Portugal in 2007 with an obligatory three-day waiting period. Indeed, the conflict between the traditions of the church and the modern needs of the economy are a worry for the staunchly religious Portuguese.

Although 81 percent of the Portuguese will affirm that they are Catholic and that they go to church for baptisms, marriages, or funerals, there is a growing sentiment, it seems, that the church is standing between them and progress. Traditional Catholic family values have changed dramatically in Portugal. As of 2014, nearly 50 percent of all children were born to unmarried women.

Though Portugal embraces its democracy and officially has no royal family, the affinity and affection for royalty and rank remain. The descendants of King João VI are occasionally referred to as Royal Highnesses. Those families once graced with such titles as duke or count are still respected—this despite being seen in jeans and boots working their farmlands and leading ordinary lives.

Maria da Assunção Esteves was president of the Portuguese parliament from 2011 to 2015.

WOMEN'S RIGHTS

Women in Portuguese society can be separated into two groups: urban and rural. Portuguese women have attained positions of power in the fields of politics, law, and engineering, and these women usually come from urbanized areas. However, many women still consider themselves socially subordinate to men. A Commission on the Status of Women, founded in 1977 to defend women's rights, nonetheless campaigns against formidable odds to bring about greater sexual equality.

There is a common saying in Portugal that goes like this: *A mulher em casa, o homen na praça* (a-MUL-yer em KAH-sa, oh OH-men na PRAH-sa). Translated directly, it reads: "The woman at home, the man in the square." Until 1969 a husband could refuse permission for his wife to obtain her own passport. The family and society were traditionally male-dominated. It was not until 1969 that women were allowed to vote. They also gained the right to a civil divorce (not permitted by the Catholic Church), family planning facilities, and career opportunities. The revolution of 1974 brought with it reforms that were aimed at improving the position of Portuguese women.

The constitution of 1976 brought them full voting rights. In 1979, Maria de Lourdes Pintasilgo was appointed the country's first female prime minister. In 1984, abortion was made legal in exceptional circumstances, such as rape or severe fetal malformation. Even though since 2007 abortions have been legal in any circumstance until ten weeks, many Portuguese doctors still refuse to perform them. More Portuguese women are also obtaining higher education and, due in part to financial necessity, are joining the workforce. As of 2014, Portuguese women make up 31 percent of parliament. While this is still a lower percentage than it should be, it is much better than the percentage of US women in Congress, which is lower than 20 percent!

RURAL LIFE

In 2013, 38 percent of the Portuguese lived a rural life. This is down from 45 percent in 2003. Farm life used to be most common in Portugal about a decade ago, but not anymore. Urban populations are growing rapidly, and more and more rural areas are becoming urbanized. Young people leave the

A farmer plows his fields with the aid of his horse in the Alentejo.

villages in search of better opportunities in the urban areas. More are eager to experience the faster pace of life in the cities.

The annual cycle of plowing, planting, tending, and harvesting is the same each year, whether the people farm potatoes in the Minho or wheat on the Alentejo plains. Vineyards in the north and fruit orchards in the south follow a similar pattern as well. The main difference is that while the northern farms tend to be smaller and family-owned, the southern ones are more prosperous, and often linked as cooperatives.

In the extensive rural areas, the small towns look picturesque, with a half-ruined castle on a hill or an ornate shrine. The people gather in the parish church on Sundays, but on weekdays they meet in the pastry shops for gossip; in the *tascas* (TASS-cas), bars where men can get a drink; or around the school, post office, or football field. The town may lack a bookshop, but boasts a public swimming pool.

THE FISHING LIFE

In many Portuguese coastal villages there is no real harbor, so the boats must be hauled over the beach on wooden rollers. Typically, men set out in the boats, and women dry the fish in the sun and supplement the family income by selling grilled sardines. The nets are dropped clear of the surf, a mile or so offshore. Then the boats return to the beach.

Living as a subsistence fisherman is a hard life. Until 1997, there were few measures to protect these brave workers who live by the unpredictable nature of the sea. Their incomes were unstable and dependent on the amount of fish they could catch. There is a general sense that the old fisherman trade is dwindling as new changes are introduced.

AN URBAN SCHEDULE

For those in the cities, office hours are from 9 a.m. to 6 p.m., with a two-hour lunch break (from 1 to 3 p.m.). Basic amenities such as cafeterias and snack bars are provided by most Portuguese companies. Most commuters use public transportation. Taxi rides are fairly cheap by European standards.

Commuting by trains and buses is inexpensive and relatively efficient. On the roads, the people drive on the right.

Shops are usually open from 9 a.m. to 1 p.m., and again from 3 to 7 p.m. On Saturdays, all businesses shut at 1 p.m. sharp. Saturday afternoon is a time reserved for sports (mostly soccer), and Sunday is a day of rest. Some malls stay open all week as modern ways infiltrate the Portuguese lifestyle.

WEDDINGS AND SPECIAL OCCASIONS

Baptism and weddings are great family occasions. Modern marriages are not arranged, although many are surprised to learn that arranged marriages in Portugal were somewhat common until the early 1990s! Today, the young choose their partners freely.

The *namoro* (NAM-o-ro), or engagement period, often starts at a dance. The formal pattern of such dances as the *vivo* and *chula* are established by courting and matrimonial traditions. In rural areas, a girl may be engaged when she is as young as fifteen, while a boy probably when he is three or four years older. In urban areas, men and women tend to marry at a later age. Most couples have a long engagement period of at least three years, sometimes as many as seven or eight. The engagement is a formal relationship. Usually no dowry is given, only a wedding trousseau.

The Portuguese adore a traditional "white wedding" if they can afford one, and a wedding dress trimmed with exquisite Madeira lace would be the envy of all.

At the wedding ceremony, the partners administer the sacrament to each other, with an extra prayer to São Gonçalo, the patron saint of weddings. The priest is present as a witness on behalf of the church.

Funerals are solemn, of course, but after all due respect has been paid to the departed, a family reunion luncheon, with jugs of wine, follows.

EDUCATION SYSTEM

Education has been compulsory since 1911. Preschool starts at age three and is optional. All Portuguese children undergo nine years of schooling from age six to fifteen. After that, a three-year secondary education course aimed at imparting specific job skills is voluntary.

One legacy from the elitist days of Salazar is a disturbingly high level of adult illiteracy. Most of those who are illiterate are elderly women who had never been to school. Traditionally, the defined role and duty of Portuguese women was to look after the home, while education was for men.

Today, the literacy rate in Portugal is on the rise. As of 2015, 95.4 percent of the population is literate. This provides the younger, educated generation the opportunity to seek employment within Portugal or within the larger global marketplace.

Although the literacy rate in Portugal has increased substantially, the present school system is still not producing all the desired results. Compulsory schooling was increased from six to nine years. However, fewer than half the children complete their full nine years of education, as many teenagers feel the need to go to work early.

Cars and trollies fill the roads of Lisbon during rush hour.

Only recently has the minimum working age been raised from fourteen to sixteen. Another challenge facing the education system in Portugal is that the geographically widespread population requires many small schools. Portugal's 140,000 teachers lack inspiration and are poorly paid even though education traditionally claims a considerable share in the country's budget.

The demand for a university education is growing. From a mere total of five universities in 1970, the number has risen to twenty-eight (fourteen private and fourteen public). However, admission is difficult and enrollment limited. There are also colleges offering specialized training in such fields as cinema, music, and theater.

HEALTH CARE SYSTEM

Health care facilities in Portugal are not as well developed as those in other European countries. Since the 1974 revolution, the number of doctors and clinics has increased. In 1979, a National Health Service that distributes free medical care was started.

Most urban residential areas have hospitals and clinics with twenty-four-hour emergency services. Many villages often rely on the local doctor. There is no lack of medical expertise among Portugal's doctors. Professor Egas Moniz, for example, won a Nobel Prize for his work in neurosurgery. However, there are not enough medical facilities and hospitals available for the growing population. Some doctors and nurses take jobs privately to supplement their low state salaries.

There are long waiting lists for treatment, and scheduling an operation could take years. Those who can afford it visit private specialists and clinics, while those who cannot simply seek advice from their local pharmacist. In most rural areas, people rely on a combination of traditional herbal remedies and modern treatments.

Statistics show a birthrate of 9.4 (the lowest rate in sixty years) and a death rate of 10.2 out of every 1,000 Portuguese, and an infant mortality rate—the number of children who die in their first year—of 4.48 out of every 1,000 children in 2013. On average, men in Portugal live to the age of seventy-seven and women to eighty-four.

AFFORDABLE HOUSING

Concrete apartment blocks are appearing in Portugal, but the bulk of the domestic architecture still retains its local character. In northern Portugal, most houses are made of granite. Animals, equipment, and the wine cellar are kept on the ground floor, and a staircase outside each house leads to the living quarters on the upper floor. The houses in the central region are designed differently. The staircase is built inside each house; the walls are likely to be whitewashed; and the roofs are made of red tiles. On the Alentejo plains, most houses are single-storied and gleaming white. In the Algarve, they are also white, often with two features of Arab origin: a lace-like chimney and a roof terrace flapping with laundry.

Portugal was the first country to declare in its constitution in 1976 that "everyone shall have the right to a dwelling of adequate size satisfying standards of hygiene and comfort, and preserving personal and family privacy." However, there is a persistent shortage of low-cost housing. In the back streets of Lisbon and Porto living conditions are appalling and the poverty is startling. Thousands live in poorly built wooden shacks without proper plumbing or drainage systems.

Traditional houses are built into the granite hills of Monsanto.

INTERNET LINKS

www.biography.com/people/groups/portuguese
Here are the collected profiles of the most famous Portuguese in history.

www.cite.gov.pt/asstscite/downloads/publics/BA3113937ENC.pdf
This is the European Parliament's policy on gender equality in Portugal, which was published in 2013.

www.globalpost.com/dispatch/news/regions/europe/140515/31-reasons-you-should-move-lisbon
A fun article that lists the thirty-one reasons you should move to Lisbon right now!

www.kwintessential.co.uk/resources/global-etiquette/portugal.html
Kwintessential provides a useful guide on Portuguese customs, manners, and culture.

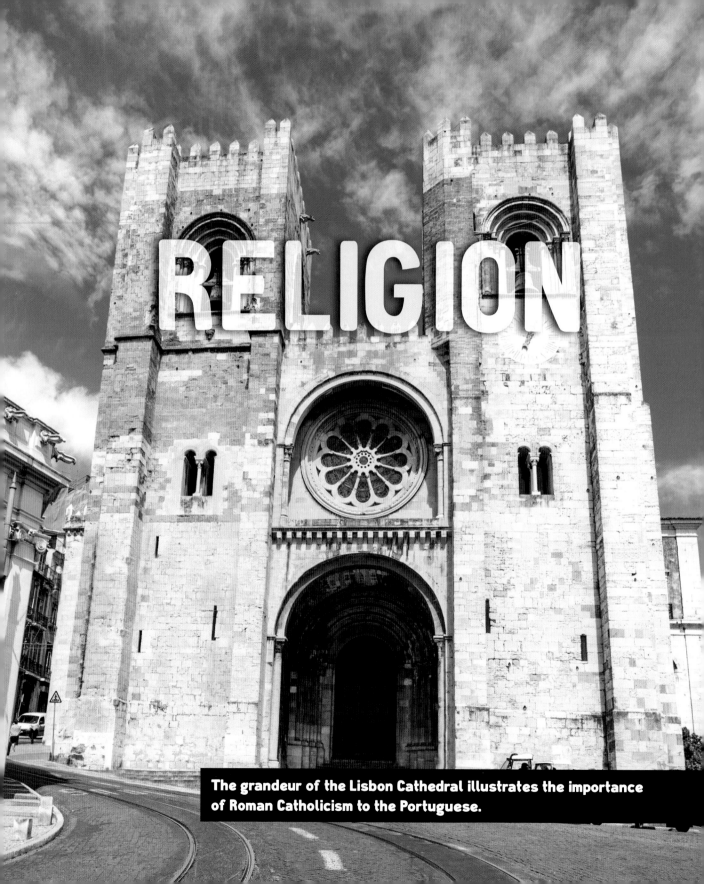

RELIGION

The grandeur of the Lisbon Cathedral illustrates the importance of Roman Catholicism to the Portuguese.

8

ALTHOUGH THERE IS NO OFFICIAL religion in Portugal, the Portuguese hold a deep respect for the Roman Catholic Church. In recent years, the percent of Portuguese people who consider themselves Catholic has been declining—from 92 percent in 2005 to 81 percent in 2015. Less than 20 percent of the population state that they attend mass regularly. Yet the Catholic faith still dominates many aspects of Portuguese life: family gatherings and holidays, feast days and weddings often follow the structure of religious celebration.

Catholicism is still more prevalent today in rural areas than in big cities. In fact, the importance of religion is immediately evident to anyone visiting a small Portuguese town: the church dominates the layout of the town, either standing on a hilltop or in the main square. Saints' days and religious holidays are still regularly celebrated in more rural areas.

Before the revolution of 1974, non-Catholics were not able to freely practice their religion in Portugal without restrictions. Since then, however, all people have the right to practice whatever religion they

"Where is God, even if he doesn't exist? I want to pray and to weep, to repent of crimes I didn't commit, to enjoy the feeling of forgiveness like a caress that's more than maternal."
–Fernando Pessoa, *The Book of Disquiet*

choose. Non-Catholic religious groups in Portugal make up only 5 percent of the total population and include Protestants, Muslims, Hindus, and Jews. Approximately 5 percent of the population considers themselves irreligious, agnostic, or atheist—a number that is growing rapidly.

RELIGIOUS FREEDOM

Present-day Portugal enjoys official freedom of worship. The vast majority of the people are Roman Catholics. Most other beliefs—like those of the Jews, Protestants, and Muslims—are tolerated. The word "tolerated" is important, for there was a long period of time during which there was no religious tolerance.

The tortures of the Spanish Inquisition are infamous, but few people are aware of the horrors of the Portuguese Inquisition. Directed originally at the converted Jews known as New Christians, the Inquisition increased in power until it virtually ruled the country. Strict Catholicism became the state religion and remained so until 1911.

In keeping with the Catholic practice worldwide, the Portuguese consider the Virgin Mary, the mother of Jesus, as a friend and protector. Nossa Senhora

A traditional Easter parade winds through the streets of an Alentejo town.

SAINT ELIZABETH

Elizabeth of Portugal (1271–1336) was once queen of Portugal and is today venerated as a Roman Catholic saint. Elizabeth's father, Peter III, was king of Aragon—a now autonomous region in northeastern Spain. A marriage between her and King Dinis of Portugal was arranged when she was just ten years old. At the royal court, she got in trouble for devoting her life to the sick and poor. Many others in the court felt that Elizabeth's simple and pious way of life made their own extravagant lifestyles look bad.

King Dinis forbade his wife from sneaking out of the palace to minister to the poor. One day, as Elizabeth was crossing the courtyard with bread in the apron of her dress to give the poor, Dinis caught her. He asked her what she was carrying in her apron, ready to punish her for disobeying his wishes. "I'm only carrying roses, my lord," she told her husband. When Dinis ordered her to show him, Elizabeth obeyed. Inside her apron, the bread had turned into roses, and Saint Elizabeth has been known for this miracle ever since.

(noss-a sen-YOR-a) is Our Lady, whom the faithful believe will surely, if prayed to devoutly, watch over a birth, a journey, an impending death, or any family event. She is also Nossa Senhora dos Navegantes (noss-a sen-YOR-a dos na-vi-GAN-tes), or Our Lady of the Navigators, guardian of the sailors. She and the saints provide a way of sending petitions to God, who is generally considered too distant and powerful to be approached directly.

Nearly all Portuguese call themselves devout Roman Catholics. The Catholic faith also forms the basis of many Portuguese festivals, in which processions, prayers, singing, dancing, bullfights, and fireworks mark the celebrations.

Despite the people's religious ways, superstitious customs still linger in many communities. Yet the church remains the central meeting place of the parish, and Sunday services and religious festivals are looked upon as an opportunity for family and friends to gather for a good time of fellowship and to catch up on the latest news.

At Easter, the cross is taken from the church to be kissed in each house in the parish, a symbol of the new life to be shared by all.

PILGRIMAGES

There is a general belief that devout prayers to particular saints will yield answers to certain problems and specific requests. It would be correct, for example, to pray to Saint Lawrence if one suffered from a toothache, or to Saint Bráz to ask for a cure to a sore throat. Saint Christopher is specifically concerned with travelers, and Our Lady of the Conception with infertility. Nazaré has a chapel that was built by a twelfth-century knight, Fuas Roupinho, to honor Our Lady of Nazareth, who saved him from falling over a cliff while he was pursuing a buck on horseback. Visitors are shown "the very hoofmark" at the edge of the drop. In certain places, national shrines are constructed where prayers to certain saints seem to be answered more readily. Pilgrimages to such shrines are a feature of Portuguese faith.

When a prayer is answered, the saint must be thanked, or one may incur some heavenly displeasure. Such expressions of gratitude often take the form of a wax offering in the shape of the organ cured, or gifts of money, jewelry, flowers, or even discarded crutches or glasses where these are appropriate. At Fátima, which is probably the most favored shrine in the country, so many votive offerings are presented that a special furnace is needed to burn them.

Of the many sacred pilgrimages, that to Bom Jesus (bon SHAY-sus)—the Good Jesus—is perhaps the most spectacular. In the woods overlooking Braga (in the Minho), this pilgrimage church of the north is reached by a great zigzag granite staircase that pilgrims climb on their knees, although an option for the less able is also available.

Another place of pilgrimage in the north is Penha, a sacred mountain beside Guimarães. Here among weird rock formations is an enormous statue of Pope Pius X. On a great boulder nearby is a carved memorial to Sacadura Cabral and Gago Coutinho, the two Portuguese aviators who pioneered transatlantic flying.

Tourists, rather than pilgrims, cross the plains of the Alentejo to visit the church of Saint Francis. In the town of Évora lies the grim Capela dos Ossos (KAP-el dos OSS-os)—the Chapel of Bones. Matched bones and skulls from five thousand skeletons line the walls, while carved above the doorway is an eerie reminder, "We bones that are here await yours." There are other chapels like this in Portugal.

OUR LADY OF FÁTIMA

Near Leiria, toward the center of Portugal, stands one of the largest shrines in western Europe. There, on May 13, 1917, three shepherd children saw a vision of the Virgin Mary. A lady

The haunting interior of the Chapel of Bones in Évora.

"brighter than the sun," dressed in a white gown and veil, spoke to them out of an oak tree and told them to return on the thirteenth day of each month until October.

Although the local authorities disapproved of this story, the Virgin Mary is said to have returned each month with messages of peace and advice to pray regularly. On October 13, seventy thousand pilgrims waited with the three children. Many affirmed afterward that miraculous beams of sunlight shone across the sky, curing illnesses and bringing sight to the blind, but only the children saw their vision for the last time.

Fátima is now the center of religious devotion in Portugal. Vast crowds gather on the thirteenth of each month, and hundreds of thousands gather in May and October. Faithful visitors cross the huge esplanade on their knees to present their prayers at the Chapel of the Apparitions.

PORTUGUESE JEWS

Jews first settled in Portugal in the time of the Moors. Many became rich and contributed to the country as bankers and financiers. Some sixty thousand more arrived when Spain expelled its Jews in 1492. However, with the arrival of the Inquisition, first in Spain and then in Portugal, thousands were tortured and others burned to death for public entertainment. During one night in 1506, nearly four thousand Jews in Lisbon were put to the sword.

Traces of the Jewish quarter, Judiaria, can still be found in many towns. The most famous is in Castelo de Vide, where Portugal's oldest synagogue, founded in the thirteenth century, is tucked away in a narrow, cobbled street. There is a fifteenth-century synagogue in Tomar. It was declared a national monument in 1921 and is now a museum containing evidence of Tomar's ancient Jewish community. The high-ceilinged hall is often used for concerts and cultural activities.

The narrow streets of a traditional Jewish quarter in Castelo de Vide, Portugal.

The largest Jewish community in Portugal numbers about five hundred and resides in Belmonte, close to the national park of the Serra da Estrela near the northern border. In Castelo Branco, a statue stands in honor of Amato Lusitano, a respected sixteenth-century Jewish doctor of medicine. There is a strong Jewish community in this part of Portugal.

The Jewish community is also witnessing an increase in numbers thanks to the Portuguese government. In 2013, the parliament announced that it would offer a citizenship process to any descendant of a Sephardic Jewish relative who had left Portugal under persecution during the Portuguese Inquisition. In 2015, the extent of citizenship expanded to include any person who could trace their history to the Sephardic Jewish line, through one's last name, language, or lineage (whether direct or indirect). As of 2015, citizenship applications were being accepted and processed.

CARETO

Of all the ancient customs in Portugal one of the oldest is the Careto tradition. Every year on Fat Sunday and Shrove Tuesday, young men wear wooden masks, costumes made of yellow, red, and green fringed wool, and bells around their waist, and run around their villages making noise and trying to find young, unmarried women to dance with them. The masks allow the men to remain anonymous and to dance without worrying how they must look. Sometimes the tradition includes fake weddings between these young men and women, which are done in good humor and don't last beyond the day. The next morning, the young man is allowed to visit the girl he "married" the previous day and receive food and wine from the girl's family in gratitude. This tradition is rooted in Celtic culture but has been adapted to the Catholic religious ceremonies of Lent.

RELIGIOUS BELIEFS AND SUPERSTITIONS

Portuguese Catholics are staunch Christians and profoundly superstitious at the same time. Each region has its favorite beliefs, such as that werewolves can be heard howling in the mountains or that the father's pants should be draped over the crib to protect a newborn from witches.

On All Saints' Day, lamps are lit and tombs are cleaned, decorated with flowers, and visited by relatives. Commemorating their ancestors links people with the past as they pray together for the dead. In the northwest, some people say they can see a ghostly vision of a "procession of the dead," in which those who have died most recently go past carrying a coffin containing the ghost of the person who will be the next to die. The "seers" dare not reveal any names because it is believed that they will join the procession if they do so.

A religious *festa* (FES-ta), or celebration, could include a procession of priests, choirboys, and servers carrying candles and images of saints. These processions are also accompanied with exploding rockets to frighten off devils.

THE ENCHANTED MOURA

According to Portuguese fairy tales, the moura encantada, *or enchanted moura, are supernatural female beings who guard castles, mountains, rivers, and even treasures. They lie in wait for a human to stumble upon them and promise the treasure they are guarding to whomever can release them from the spell they are under. Oftentimes, these beautiful maidens are depicted combing their long hair with golden combs.*

The enchanted moura are part of the race of mouros, *supernatural guardians who have populated Portugal since the beginning of time. Stories of these supernatural beings are thought to have been handed down from the original Celtic tribes that inhabited the Iberian Peninsula before the Romans. Today, almost every Portuguese village has its own story of a moura or mouro, the treasures they guard, and the fortunate or unfortunate humans who discovered them.*

Shrines with an image of Jesus, the Virgin Mary, or a local saint are found along many country roads. They are there to protect travelers or perhaps to celebrate an answered prayer. Carved along the bottom of the shrine may be little flames around wretched figures that represent the souls of sinners suspended in purgatory.

FOLKTALES AND TRADITIONS

South of Guarda (the highest city in Portugal), in the Serra da Estrela mountains, is a ring of towering crags of such daunting shapes that the town in their center has been called Sortelha, meaning "magic ring." Local superstition still renders it the home of witches and werewolves. In the Vale de Nogueives (in the Trás-os-Montes), huge carved stones are believed to have been altars used for pre-Christian human sacrifice.

Folk in mountain villages often burn huge yule logs in front of their doorways or by the church porch on Christmas Eve to ensure that there will be a warm place for the Christ child to be born and also to ensure that the poorest people will not be cold on that night.

On the coast north of Porto is the small harbor of Ofir. This is the site of one of Portugal's more extravagant religious legends, based on the biblical figure of King Solomon. Folklore claims that King Solomon used to come ashore here to collect gold from the inland mines. The gold was the source of much of his fabulous wealth and was used generously to adorn his temples. In gratitude, he sent a shipload of his finest horses to Ofir, but the vessel was wrecked before it could reach land. As the horses sank beneath the waves, they were turned into stone. This may explain why Ofir is a popular spot for underwater diving!

Supposedly magical cliffs surround the medieval castle of Sortelha (pictured here).

INTERNET LINKS

www.fatima.org/essentials/facts/story1.asp
Look at the photos that accompany this description of the Virgin Mary apparitions at Fátima.

www.mpjh.org/Welcome.html
Learn more about the Museum of Portuguese Jewish History, based in Lisbon, here.

www.santuario-fatima.pt/portal/index.php?lang=EN
This is the official site for Our Lady of Fátima, where you can read more about the apparition of the Lady of the Rosary.

LANGUAGE

A mural depicts *fado* performances in the streets of Lisbon.

PORTUGUESE IS A ROMANCE language, which means that, like French and Spanish, it is derived from Latin. Although it is not widely spoken in the rest of Europe, Portuguese is the most spoken language in South America.

The Romans brought their language with them to the Iberian Peninsula in 210 BCE. It quickly became the dominant language above the Celtic languages that had been used in the region before, and was used for administration and trade. Following the Moorish invasion in the eighth century, Arabic became the dominant language in the conquered regions, although Christian groups still spoke a variant of the Romance language that would become Portuguese.

Toward the end of the thirteenth century, King Dinis set up the first university in Portugal, and this helped establish Portuguese as the national language following the collapse of Muslim rule in Europe. Old Portuguese thrived during the Middle Ages and developed into the modern Portuguese spoken today around the sixteenth century. Modern Portuguese evolved from dialects of Latin but also incorporates French and Arabic vocabulary.

LANGUAGE EVOLUTION

Language is thought in action, according to the great Portuguese poet Fernando Pessoa. Portuguese goes beyond being the language of a corner of Europe; three centuries ago, it was the tongue of trade of most of the ports of South America, India, and southwestern Asia.

There was a time when Portuguese and Spanish were virtually the same language. Then, in the twelfth century, Portugal broke away from Spanish control, and its language evolved on its own with distinctively different sounds and different grammatical characterizations.

Portuguese appeared as a separate language after the thirteenth century. As with other languages, it remained alive and continued evolving. As lands were discovered or colonized by Portuguese explorers, new expressions were added to the language. Even in this century, terms from French and English (mainly technical or concerning sports) have been adopted and added to Portuguese vocabulary.

Portuguese is correctly termed a Romance language, meaning it developed from Latin (like French, Italian, and Spanish). For scholars and linguists, the Portuguese spoken at Coimbra is accepted as the language at its best. Smooth and musical, it has an elaborate sentence structure. It is, for many, the ideal language of lyric poetry, melancholy and sweet. Some say that Portuguese language and literature reached their richest development in the *Lusiads* (dealing with the voyage of Vasco da Gama) and other works of Luís Vaz de Camões—in the same way others claim English was at its zenith in the works of William Shakespeare.

There is a wide range of local accents. The northern Portuguese, long cut off in their mountain villages, speak a dialect that the rest of the country finds hard to understand. The tiny village of Rio do Onor on the northern border with Spain has developed its own dialect, music, and folk dances. Those who live in Lisbon can hardly understand the people of Algarve, where many speak some English.

From the beginning of the twentieth century, there were calls to simplify and standardize Portuguese spelling. In 1953 the governments of Portugal and Brazil approved a new system: *f* was substituted for *ph*, *t* for *th*, and *i* for *y*.

PORTUGUESE AROUND THE WORLD

The language of Portugal is also the language of Brazil, Angola, Mozambique, Cape Verde, São Tomé and Principe, East Timor, and Guinea-Bassau. Portuguese is the base tongue from which many Creole languages have grown. There are large communities of Portuguese speakers in the United States, France, Venezuela, and South Africa. It is the seventh most widely spoken language in the world.

There are four recognized Portuguese dialects: those of northern, central, and southern Portugal, and the Brasiliero of Brazil that has had added input from the Tupi indigenous tribes and African slaves. About two million people in northwestern Spain speak the northern Portuguese dialect called Galician.

On their own mainland, almost all Portuguese understand Spanish in addition to their own language. Children are taught both French and English. Although shopkeepers and tour guides show off their linguistic abilities, most Portuguese expect visitors to learn a little Portuguese. How else can the courtesies of greeting be exchanged?

This engraving of Luís Vaz de Camões depicts the national poet circa 1790.

Hello	*Ola (OH-lah)*
Good morning	*Bom dia (bawng DEE-er)*
Good evening	*Boa noite (boa-er NAWNG-ter)*
Thank you	*Obrigado (oh-bri-GAR-doh) for men; women say Obrigada*
Please	*Por favor (poor fa-VO-ar)*
Yes	*Sim (SEE-ng)*
No	*Não (NAH-ng)*
Goodbye	*Adeus (er-DAY-oos)*
Come back soon	*Até breve (er-TAY BRAY-ver)*

PRONUNCIATION

The pronunciation of Portuguese words is very different from their written form. The syllable to be stressed is not always the first syllable—*Setúbal*, for example, is pronounced "sh-TOO-bl." Portuguese has nasalized vowels, somewhat similar to French. Syllables ending with *m* and *n* often sound as if they ended with *ng*. So *sim* (yes) is pronounced "SEE-ng," but without sounding the *g*. The same sort of sound is created by the tilde accent (that wavy line over a vowel), as in ã, ão, and ães. So *não* (no) is pronounced "NAH-ng," also without sounding the *g*.

The cedilla accent, ç, comes under a *c* and gives it a soft sound. So *graça* (grace) is pronounced "GRASS-ah." If the *c* does not have a cedilla, it sounds hard. So *pico* (top) is pronounced "PEE-koh." *S* sounds like *sh* before a consonant or at the end of a word. Thus *Cascais* is pronounced "KAHS-kaish." This gives Portuguese a rather slushy sound. The letter *j* sounds like the *s* in the word "pleasure." The letter *g* often sounds the same as *j*, unless followed by *a* or *o*, in which case it sounds hard.

GREETINGS AND MANNERS

Traditional courtesy is a strong feature of Portuguese communication. Everyone expects to be treated with dignity. Greetings and manners tend to be elaborate. "Your Excellency" is a common form of address. Lawyers, doctors, and university graduates are addressed respectfully as *Senhor Doutor* (SEN-yor DOO-tor) for men, and *Senhora Doutora* (sen-YOR-a doo-TOR-a") for women. Even such titles as *Excelentíssimo Senhor* (EX-se-len-TISS-i-mo SEN-yor) or *Excelentíssima Senhora* (EX-se-len-TISS-i-ma sen-YOR-a) are used widely.

Despite such courtesies being widespread, there is an underlying obstinacy among some people to ignore them—or to allow their more modern-minded children to do so. There is a Portuguese expression, *por se suas tamanquinhas* (por se SOO-as ta-man-KEEN-as), which means "to put on your clogs," in other words, to move slowly or to be obstinate. This comes from the leather country boots called *tamancas* (ta-MAN-kas), which have a thick wooden sole.

INTERNET LINKS

www.bbc.co.uk/languages/portuguese
The BBC offers free lessons and online courses in Portuguese.

www.golisbon.com/practical-lisbon/language.html
This is a good resource for learning the basics of Portuguese, including interesting trivia about the language.

www.omniglot.com/writing/portuguese.htm
At this useful site, you can learn not only the history of the Portuguese language but also important vocabulary.

ARTS

Men sing the traditional cante Alentejo during a parade

THE PORTUGUESE ARE PROUD OF their artistic heritage, and for good reason. Their culture has found expression in music, literature, painting, and singing, as well as in handicrafts. But Portugal's national treasure is fado, the woeful folksongs of Lisbon and the Alentejo. In fact, UNESCO, a UN organization that protects peace in the international community through collaboration in education, science, and culture, recently named fado music as one of the world's intangible cultural treasures.

Yet another one of Portugal's intangible cultural treasures is the *cante* Alentejo, a form of polyphonic singing from the Alentejo region. Choral groups are divided into the *ponto* section, or the lower range, and the *alto* section, or the higher range, to sing these traditional folksongs. Lyrical traditional poetry is often set to melodies, which are sung without instrumentation.

Finally, craft workers in small villages across Portugal have perfected traditional crafts that vary depending on the region. The know-how to create these masterpieces has been passed down through generations, and oftentimes its origin is lost in time. These crafts include the decorated linen of Guimarães, intricate baskets of the Algarve, richly carved ox-yokes from the Minho, pottery made from black clay, intricate and vibrantly colored paper flowers, and stoneware with the Portuguese emblem of the cockerel. All of these crafts are testimonies to the skills—and unique cultures—of the craft workers.

THE ROOSTER OF BARCELOS

A popular legend relates how a pilgrim on his way to Compostela in Spain was accused and found guilty of theft as he left the Portuguese town of Barcelos. He was sentenced to the gallows, all the while proclaiming his innocence and praying to Saint James. His last desperate cry for justice included a claim that a roast fowl on the judge's dinner table would rise and crow as proof to his innocence. The bird duly and miraculously returned to life, crowing loudly and sparing the man his life. The rooster of Barcelos has become one of the most common emblems of Portugal, and you can find it engraved on many Portuguese handicrafts.

The rooster of Barcelos is the traditional symbol of Portugal.

LITERATURE

The songs made up by traveling minstrels in the Middle Ages paved the way for the birth of Portuguese literature, for each song combines a well-informed commentary on the events of the day with an appreciation of style and wordplay. Poetry, in its different styles, has always been appreciated in Portugal. In the fifteenth century, court chroniclers began to record Portuguese history, but all books were still handwritten. It was the revolutionary invention of printing, at the start of the Renaissance, which allowed literature to expand and flourish.

The many plays of Gil Vicente established Portuguese theater, making religious dramas rooted in medieval style, mysterious tragicomedies with historical themes, and broad comic satires poking fun at everyday life in sixteenth-century Portugal mainstays in the Portuguese arts scene. Poets experimented with the Italian sonnet form. Luís Vaz de Camões was among the leading poets and is remembered most for his patriotic *Lusiads*. The excitement of exploration and sea discovery is reflected in much Portuguese writing.

In the eighteenth century, the Enlightenment spread through Europe, evoking fresh perspectives on education and science. In Portugal, neoclassicism became popular, advocating a return to the pure power of language in reaction to the exaggerated verbiage of the seventeenth-century baroque. Among such social commentary came the satirical poetry of Manuel Maria Barbosa du Bocage, who lived riotously and wrote irreverently. Romanticism followed, with the lively plays and novels of Almeida Garrett and the historical novels and poems of Alexandre Herculano. The romantic ideal in Portugal created a cultural rebirth in the country.

Scholarly argument from the university town of Coimbra resulted in the publication of *Bom Senso e do Bom Gosto* (*Good Sense and Good Taste*), a now famous discussion of late nineteenth-century literary attitudes. Hans Christian Andersen visited Portugal in 1866 and considered the country "the stuff of fairy tales."

The word "saudade"—a sad longing for the past—best describes the mood and style of most Portuguese writing. Fernando Pessoa, one of Portugal's greatest poets, indulged often in this nationalistic nostalgia in his works. By using various pen names, he could be romantic, wry, heroic, or comic—all styles used in his writing.

Portugal is proud of its authors. Famous names include José Eça de Queiroz, a novelist with wit, invention, and a polished style; and Fernando Namora, an internationally famous novelist. Also famous are Alves Redol, whose book *Gaibeus*, about the harsh life of migrant laborers, has gone into its seventeenth reprinting; the Nobel Prize—winning novelist José Saramago; Almada Negreiros, poet and painter; Viterino Nemésio, whose novel *Mau Tempo no Canal* (*Bad Weather in the Channel*), written in 1944, is still considered outstanding; and the nonconformist poet Manuel Alegre.

Unfortunately, reading is not a popular pastime in Portugal. Books are costly and a luxury for people who are struggling to make a living. Such showpiece libraries as the baroque fantasy in Coimbra University seem to have books on display for their impressive bindings rather than for actual reading.

Fernando Pessoa (1888–1935) is considered one of Portugal's greatest poets and a major figure in twentieth-century literature. He worked not only as a poet but also as a translator, literary critic, and even a publisher, and wrote in Portuguese, English, and French. Born in Lisbon, Pessoa spent much of his youth living in Durban, South Africa, with his family, before returning to Portugal for his studies.

Pessoa is best known for Message, *an epic made up of forty-four short poems, and* The Book of Disquiet, *which has been called a fragmentary autobiography. Pessoa's works were written under many heteronyms—a word that Pessoa invented to mean the various different characters he invented. Rather than using his own name, Pessoa would write and publish books as these different heteronyms such as Alberto Caeiro, Richard Reis, and Alvaro de Campos. Each of these different characters had different backgrounds, writing styles, and political opinions, and Pessoa used more than seventy of them! Unfortunately, Pessoa's works did not receive widespread attention until after his death.*

THEATER AND FILM

Due to the competition from movies and television, the once proud theatrical tradition of Portugal has faded, dependent almost totally on subsidies offered by the Theater Fund and the generous Calouste Gulbenkian Foundation. In the 1950s, the Porto Experimental Theater worked valiantly to maintain live theater productions in Portugal. Then, in 1974, the abolition of censorship enabled theater groups to aim at a new popular audience.

The first Portuguese film was made in 1896, and determined producers have continued to fight for popular support and official subsidies. Box office records are held by António-Pedro Vasconcelos's *O Lugar do Morte* (*Place of Death*), which attracted 130,000 viewers in 1984. Still, up until the 1990s, an average of twelve films were produced each year by Portuguese filmmakers, most of whom usually made one film a decade. The local market for movies is small—there are only about five hundred movie theaters in the whole country, although large cinemas are becoming popular. Portuguese cinematography is hailed as unique and innovative. Portugal's most respected filmmaker is Manoel de Oliveira.

Born in 1908, Manoel de Oliveira was the oldest known active director and worked until his death in April 2015. His work is often punctuated with social messages. For example, his first film, *Douro*, produced in 1931, is a silent documentary about the harsh conditions of agricultural life in the city of his birth, Porto. It was not warmly received by his fellow countrymen at first, but the film gradually earned praise as avant-garde cinema. His films deal with his favorite themes of Portuguese life, religion, and history, some focusing heavily on psychological drama and dialogue.

Oliveira was inactive during the years of dictatorship in Portugal. The peak of his career came in the 1970s when he was established as a notable director. From the 1990s until 2015, he directed an average of one film per year.

ARCHITECTURAL STYLES

Portugal offers Celtic fortifications, Roman temples, a handful of Moorish buildings, many Arab-influenced structures, medieval castles, and churches in every style from stern Gothic to encrusted Baroque.

As Christianity recaptured the peninsula, churches were built in the Romanesque style then popular in Europe. Constructed mostly out of carved granite, the churches have simple architectural features, such as semicircular arches and smooth round pillars, and often a cross-shaped plan to the building. The pointed Gothic arch became popular in the thirteenth and fourteenth centuries, giving the cathedrals added height and increased elegance and gracefulness.

A combination of Romanesque, Manueline, and Renaissance architecture can be seen in the Convent of Christ overlooking Tomar on the plains northeast of Lisbon. Built first as a castle, this was the headquarters of the Knights Templar, a religious order originally founded to fight the Muslims and protect the Holy Sepulchre in Jerusalem. However, their military strength soon became a threat in Europe, and they were expelled from France and Spain. Many took refuge in Portugal, where in 1320 King Dinis gave them a

Such terms as "Romanesque" and "Gothic" are used to describe architectural styles all over Europe, but only in Portugal will you find the Manueline style of architecture. Named after King Manuel I, in whose reign the style came to its peak, this is almost oceanic art with exuberant yet delicate decoration that stems from the worldwide exploration by the Portuguese in the fifteenth and sixteenth centuries. Its main feature is stone carving that links maritime themes with motifs from heraldry and Moorish design. Pillars twist like barley sugar in the fashion of ship's cables, and buildings are decorated with a profusion of ropes, knots, anchors, globes, pearls, shells, and the military cross of the Order of Christ.

The Manueline influence is reflected in the Monastery of Jerónimos (right), a monument containing the tombs of Camões and Vasco da Gama. It can also be seen in the Batalha Monastery (Monastery of the Battle), built to commemorate victory over the Spaniards at Aljubarrota in 1385. Prince Henry the Navigator is buried there among fantastic carved traceries, like lace made of stone.

new title, the Order of Christ. After the king's death, they lost their military status and became monks.

Portuguese architecture next adopted the exuberance of the Baroque, closely associated with King João V. This found expression in gilded woodwork, ranges of stairways (as at Bom Jesus in Braga), twisting pillars, and a colorful use of *azulejos* (a-zoo-LAY-shoss), or ceramic tiles.

Toward the end of the eighteenth century, a neoclassical style with Greek and Roman colonnades became popular, but the Portuguese love for the romantic still found expression in such unique buildings as the Disney-like Palace of Pena in Sintra, and the wildly ornate Palace Hotel of Bussaco. A few equally unusual Art Nouveau buildings emerged in the early twentieth century, mostly in Lisbon and Coimbra.

VISUAL ARTS

Much of the early art and sculpture of Portugal was religious in subject as the Catholic Church was the great patron of the arts. Groups of three painted panels called triptychs, intended to stand behind an altar, show saints and biblical scenes. Sometimes the faces of donors who provided funds for the building of the church or the creation of the artwork were painted among a watching crowd. Carvings inside and outside churches and on royal tombs, such as the gilded woodwork in the Church of São Francisco in Porto, are impressive.

As politics took center stage, sculptors created commemorative monuments and artists turned to celebratory portraits. No visitor to Lisbon can fail to be impressed by Leopoldo de Almeida's *Monument to the Discoveries*, showing Prince Henry the Navigator at the front of a lineup of famous Portuguese explorers.

Portugal's greatest painter, Vieira Portuense, expressed himself as a neoclassicist, while painter Domingos António Sequeira produced dramatic, almost mystical works in the romantic style. Columbano Pinheiro was a masterly portrait painter in the early twentieth century, and his brother Rafael set up a porcelain factory that became a school for ceramicists. Today, Portugal's well-renowned artists include painters Julio Pomar, Paula Rego, and the late Vieira da Silva; sculptors José de Guimarães; and architect Jorge Mealha.

CRAFTS AND DECORATIVE ARTS

Any country that has been occupied by Muslim conquerors seems to inherit an appreciation and skill for geometric decoration. The greatest national art form of Portugal is probably the glazed tiles (azulejos) that adorn walls everywhere. Other skills include the making of delicate gold jewelry, exquisite furniture with gilt engraving and Oriental details, blue and white porcelain from Aveiro in imitation of imported Chinese ceramics, rare Arraiolos carpets influenced by Persian design, and striking stained glass.

Every local market in Portugal displays crafts, whether hand-painted pottery, tapestry cushions, wall hangings, copper coffeepots, or beautifully shaped baskets.

AZULEJOS

There is a national passion for covering the walls of buildings—churches, palaces, restaurants, and railway stations—with blue and white ceramic tiles. Even ordinary houses are covered with striking tiled designs. The use of decorative tiles was introduced to Portugal by the Moors. The name "azulejos" comes from the Arabic al zuleiq *(ahl zoo-LAYK), meaning "a small polished stone." Though some are multicolored and some more classical, with white backgrounds and feathery gilded borders, the favorite colors remain white and blue (colors introduced by Dutch artisans). Clay in square molds is fired at high temperatures, then painted with oxides: copper for green, cobalt for blue, antimony for yellow, manganese for brown, and tin for white. There is a National Tile Museum in Lisbon showing the history and changing skills of making azulejos.*

MUSEUMS

Portugal, particularly Lisbon, is rich with heritage and has many museums. The pride of them all is the Calouste Gulbenkian Museum, built to house and display the thousands of priceless objects and works of art collected by the Armenian millionaire and given to his adopted country. The collection ranges from Egyptian ceramics and gold coins from ancient Greece, through medieval manuscripts and tapestries, to paintings by Rembrandt, Watteau, Turner, Manet, and Renoir. There is also Chinese porcelain and French Art Nouveau. In addition, the building houses a concert hall, library, and snack bar. Lisbon's other museums cover interests in ancient, modern, decorative, folk, and religious art; archaeology; military and naval matters; and azulejos.

MUSIC

The chants of church worship, the songs of troubadours, and singers at the royal court were integral to the growth of music and traditional dance forms in Portugal. King João V, rich with gold from Brazil, hired a group of Italian singers to perform under the direction of composer Domenico Scarlatti, thereby heralding the arrival of opera in Lisbon. In the eighteenth century, the performances of João Domingos Bomtempo created greater Portuguese interest in the music of Haydn, Mozart, and Beethoven. John Philip Sousa, whose father was a Portuguese immigrant, made his name in the United States by composing marches such as "Stars and Stripes Forever" and inventing the musical instrument known as the sousaphone.

Among Portugal's more modern composers are Luís de Freitas Branco and Fernando Lopes Graça. There is a National Broadcasting Symphony Orchestra in Lisbon. The Portuguese enjoy concerts, and these are often staged in cathedrals, palaces, and ruined castles. The concert might feature a popular pianist such as Artur Pizarro.

INTERNET LINKS

museu.gulbenkian.pt/Museu/en/Homepage
The official site of the Calouste Gulbenkian Museum in English.

www.poetryfoundation.org/bio/fernando-pessoa
This introduction to the important Portuguese poet Fernando Pessoa includes some of his most famous poems.

sacred-texts.com/neu/lus/index.htm
You can read the full text of the *Lusiads* in English here.

www.worldmusic.net/guide/portugal
This is an in-depth guide to traditional Portuguese music with clips and videos.

LEISURE

Fadistas play their evocative songs at the Jerónimos Monastery.

11

THE PORTUGUESE ARE FAMOUS FOR living life at a more leisurely pace. Stores are closed daily during the midday siesta time, and most are also closed early on Saturday and all of Sunday. Meals are enjoyed slowly. In Portugal, food is to be enjoyed as a drawn-out social activity among friends and family. Holidays and festivals are frequently celebrated, and if a holiday falls on a Tuesday or a Thursday, the Portuguese take an extra-long weekend away from work.

Playing sports, attending soccer matches, strolling through the many parks and gardens, or taking in a fado concert are all favorite leisure activities for the Portuguese. The Portuguese also enjoy drinking wine. Portugal's wine consumption per capita ranks among the highest in the world. Once, it was considered improper for women in Porto to ask for port outright when in restaurants or bars. Instead, they would order "cold tea," which was code for port—brought to them secretly in a teapot! Today, there are no such restrictions for women. For young people, the legal drinking age in Portugal is sixteen for beer and wine and eighteen for liquor.

Loyal Portuguese fans show their love of soccer.

SPORTING LIFE

The Portuguese take part in various sports either as participants or spectators. To be adventurous in sports became a national characteristic centuries ago. For example, in 1709, Bartolomeu de Gusmão, a Jesuit priest, invented a flying machine that he named Passarola (pas-sa-ROH-la), or Big Bird. It actually rose off the ground, and the Portuguese public named him Voador (voh-AH-dorh), or the Flyer. However, his invention did not receive royal patronage, so Portugal missed the chance to become the first airborne nation. But it can claim the first air crossing of the South Atlantic in 1922. Artur de Sacadura Cabral and Gago Coutinho flew from Santa Cruz to Brazil in a tiny airplane—five years before Charles Lindbergh's more famous solo crossing in 1927.

Soccer dominates the sports scene for many men and young boys—although girls are also becoming more involved. Every season, thousands of fans pack the stadiums. Track and field and gymnastics are popular with Portuguese women.

The marathon champion Rosa Mota is a national heroine. She won the bronze medal at the Los Angeles Olympics in 1984 and became the first Portuguese woman ever to earn an Olympic medal. She did not disappoint her fans and went on to win the gold medal at the Korean Olympics in 1988. However, her early training days had been accompanied by shouts of shame, due to her dress. At that time, it was not considered correct or proper for a woman to be seen wearing shorts in public. She also relates how people used to call after her: "A woman's place is in the home. Go and cook, go and wash the dishes!" Since then, attitudes have changed, and in 1994 the Portuguese women's team won the World Cross Country Championships at Budapest.

BIGGEST WAVE EVER SURFED

Garrett McNamara is an American professional surfer who entered the Guinness World Records in 2011 when he caught the largest wave ever recorded off the coast of Nazaré in Portugal. A jet ski towed McNamara out to the wave, which was measured at 78 feet (24 m) high! The announcement of his daring feat caused some controversy until a panel of experts confirmed it at the annual Global Big Waves Awards.

But then McNamara broke his own record, catching a 100-foot (30.5 m) wave in 2013—once again in Nazaré. This isn't a coincidence; Nazaré is a world-famous spot for big-wave surfing, due to a canyon underneath the water that causes very high breaking waves. Currently, another surfer is said to have broken McNamara's world record—once again in Nazaré—although experts are waiting to confirm the height of the wave.

Among male athletes, Portugal salutes Carlos Lopes, who won the Olympic marathon in Los Angeles, and sprinter Fernando Mamede, who established a world record in the 10,000-meter (10,936-yard) dash in Stockholm, Sweden, in 1984. However, facilities for athletic training are generally lacking. There are seventeen golf courses, eleven of which are of world championship standard. Vale do Lobo and Quinta do Lago in the Algarve are perhaps the most famous, and golf is played there the whole year round. National golf championships are held twice a year. Tennis is becoming more popular, and many hotels have built clay courts for their guests in addition to the local tennis club. Water sports and ice hockey are both popular, too.

Forty-one percent of Portugal's coastline has beaches—about 500 miles (800 km) of sandy shore. Colored flags warn of strong undertows on the Atlantic coast. Polluted waters near industrial sites or on the popular Algarve, however, have no such warning systems. People must be careful when swimming or venturing to these areas. In the mountainous areas, people get to fish, hike, or go horseback riding in the cool, clean air.

For those who crave more adventure, the spirit of daring lives on. Fairly recently, a daredevil in Porto dived off the Dom Luis Bridge to break the European record for a bungee jump. With the help of a 200-foot (60 m) crane on top of the bridge, he jumped a total of 295 feet (90 m).

Car racing attracts the crowds at the Estoril Autodrome, near Lisbon, where there is an annual Formula One Grand Prix. Since 1984, many top racing teams have used the Estoril course for testing and training, and drivers like Nelson Piquet, Alan Prost, and Ayrton Senna have been regular visitors. Vila Real is the motorcycling capital of Portugal, with international events in June and July.

FUTEBOL!

Futebol (FOO-ti-bol) became popular in Portugal during the reign of King Carlos (who ascended the throne in 1889) and has become as vital to the Portuguese as baseball is to the Americans. Devoted fans fly in from far away to watch top teams Benfica or Sporting Lisbon (both of Lisbon) or FC Porto. Sporting won the Portuguese title seven times in eight years (1947–1954). Then Benfica established itself as one of Europe's finest teams in the 1960s, winning the European Cup in 1961 and 1962 and reaching the final three more

The Portuguese national soccer team lines up before a match in 2013.

times in the next six years. In 1987, Porto won the European Cup, the World Club Cup, and the European Super Cup. In 2003, Porto won the UEFA (Union of European Football Associations) Cup, the first Portuguese team to do so. In 2004, it went on to win the UEFA Champions League. Most Portuguese support one of these three teams. Of the lesser local teams, FC Guimarães offers fair competition to the big three. Two of Portugal's most famous soccer players today are Luís Figo and Cristiano Ronaldo.

In the 1928 Olympics, the Portuguese soccer team came in fifth. Portugal captured third place in the 1966 World Cup in England, came close in Mexico in 1986, and was beaten by a single goal in the last minute in the 1984 European Cup in France. In 2010, Portugal was ranked third of 205 countries by FIFA, the International Football Federation, which was its highest ranking ever.

BULLFIGHTING

The bullfights of Portugal are different from those in Spain. The main action is conducted on horseback, and it is really a contest of elegance, daring, and skill, as a *cavaleiro* (ka-val-EYR-o) controls his highly trained horse so that he can plant a dart in the bull's neck. There are different sizes of darts and different ways they can be placed.

After the cavaleiro has planted the darts, a team of eight *forcados* (for-KAH-dos) takes over on foot, wrestling the bull with their bare hands. Ever since the death of the Count of Arcos, who was gored to death in public in 1799, it has been forbidden for a bull to be killed in any fight. Instead, a gesture is made with a wooden sword to indicate the animal's defeat. However, as most bulls end up too badly wounded to survive, they are butchered out of sight afterward.

There are over thirty bullrings in Portugal. The main one is Campo Pequeno in Lisbon, built of red brick in a pseudo-Moorish style.

FADO MUSIC

This unique folk music expresses the soul of Portugal. Supposedly evolved from ballads of longing sung by homesick sailors, fado (meaning "fate") is

Amália Rodrigues is one of the most beloved Portuguese musicians of all time.

emotive and nostalgic, though not necessarily sad. It is common after dinner to sit and contemplate the glory that once was Portugal by singing or listening to fado.

The singing is full of that essential Portuguese quality, saudade, or bittersweet nostalgia. The fadista sings alone, usually accompanied by guitars—either the twelve-stringed Portuguese *guitarra* (gi-TARR-a) or the more common Western six-stringed guitar. The exception to this is fado from Coimbra. Fado in this university town is male and student-dominated and has its own unique sound using the traditional Coimbra guitar.

Amália Rodrigues was one of the most famous fado singers. She was known for her interpretations of the genre and for introducing fado to the international community. There was a great sense of national loss following her death in 1999 because she had contributed so much to the musical tradition. Another internationally famous fado singer is Mariza. Nowadays, fado is jazzed up with electronic music. Nevertheless, fado is not appreciated today by many young Portuguese, who prefer the more upbeat tempos of rock and pop. But many fado houses now cater to tourists. They levy an entrance fee, serve dinner, and charge high bar prices. Singing does not start until around 10 p.m.

TELEVISION AND RADIO

Everyone watches television, either for sports or for the soap operas, called *telenovelas* (te-li-NOH-ve-las). They watch in cafés, bars, restaurants, and homes. Television and radio licenses are paid as a percentage of the electricity bill. There are four main channels, two of which are private and the other two public. The cities also have access to cable television. Many imported programs, which are usually given Portuguese subtitles, are shown.

Radio is losing popularity in Portugal, but the elderly still listen to it, mainly in the country. Small towns have their own radio stations that play music most of the time. There are long commercial breaks at the end of every hour, causing much frustration to listeners. There are about eight radio stations, and among these, one has a Catholic focus, three are targeted at young people, and at least one is a news station.

There are eighty-nine newspapers (including seven on the Azores and four on Madeira). Nowadays, sharing information is a lot more convenient with the Internet. Portugal's English-language newspapers have gone online as well. There were 6.9 million Internet users in 2012.

INTERNET LINKS

www.mariza.com/?lang=en
The musician Marzia's official website in English.

paginas.fe.up.pt/~fado/eng/index-eng.html
This website is dedicated to educating people about fado music.

www.portugoal.net
Learn all about Portuguese football and recent matches here.

www.surfing-waves.com/atlas/europe/portugal/centro/spot/nazare.html
This is a guide to the Nazaré surf spot with information on wave quality and difficulty.

FESTIVALS

Women carry decorative baskets of bread and roses during a festival in Tomar.

12

Oorganized celebrations are a common event in Portugal, where nearly every village has its own festival or feast day and national festivals are celebrated every month. Some local festivals are small affairs, with a procession down the main street and a dinner or dance. Larger ones can last several days and include floral displays, fireworks, or bullfights. June through September is an especially busy period for these events.

Many of these festivals are religious in nature and honor a locally venerated saint. Every year during the last two weeks of June, the popular saints are celebrated during the Santos Populares festivities, which honor Saint Anthony, Saint John, and Saint Peter. These festivities take place throughout the country. In honor of Saint Elizabeth of Portugal, Portuguese women carry baskets of rose petals in Vila Franca do Lima during the Festival of Our Lady of the Roses, which has been celebrated since 1622. Another centuries-old celebration is the Corpus Christi Procession in Monção, where oxen parade next to people in the streets.

NATIONAL RELIGIOUS HOLIDAYS

Since Portugal is an overwhelmingly Catholic country, most of its national holidays are the official feast days of the Catholic Church,

"(The romarias) are the most characteristic expression of the soul of the people that you can see, and I should say the most typical merrymakings left in Europe today."
–Edward Livermore Burlingame in 1915

Musicians play during the Festival of Nossa Senhora.

some of which vary from year to year. June 10 is the main national holiday—the Day of Camões and the Community. The "Community" was added after the bloodless 1974 revolution, and the day still celebrates (as did the poet Camões) the national pride of Portugal. It is also called Portugal Day. The national anthem is "A Portuguesa," written by Lopes de Mendonça in 1890.

On April 25 the country celebrates the anniversary of the 1974 revolution. Red carnations are the symbol of this happy event because the soldiers put carnations in the barrels of their rifles. Some people still have the flowers carried on that day, carefully dried and preserved. December 1 marks Portugal's independence from Spain in 1580.

If a festival falls on a Tuesday or Thursday, many businesses also close accordingly on the Monday before or Friday after, resulting in a long weekend, known in Portugal as a *ponte* (PON-ti), or bridge.

ROMARIAS

Some people go on a *romaria* (roh-MAH-ri-a), or pilgrimage, to a shrine or sacred place to gain favor from the saint whose festival or feast day they are celebrating. At one time, pilgrims walked all the way and camped out in the woods. Now they go by bus. It is a colorful, cheerful occasion as they approach the shrine. Drums, pipes, and accordions may play; banners and floral decorations provide extra color; and there may be a special platform for dancing.

Crowds flock to Viana do Castelo (in Minho) to celebrate in the name of Nossa Senhora de Agonia (NOSS-a sen-YOR-a da a-go-NEE-a), Our Lady of Agony. For one week, women parade in widow's black or flame-colored floral costumes, and the word *amor* (a-MOR), or love, is emblazoned everywhere.

FESTIVAL OF SAINT JOHN THE BAPTIST

The Festa de São João do Porto, or the Festival of Saint John the Baptist, is an important festival that occurs every June 23 in Porto. This is the city's most important annual celebration, and it has been held in Porto for over six hundred years. Thousands of Portuguese flock to the city center in honor of Saint John the Baptist's traditional birthday. Festivities normally last until early the next morning and include delicious street food, dancing around bonfires, concerts, and a traditional releasing of lighted balloons.

This festival is intriguing because of its complex history, which blends together pagan traditions with Catholic belief. Pre-Christian courting rituals, such as bringing around cloves of garlic or leeks and hitting people in the street with them, encounter the religious iconography of the Catholic Church. It is said that if you fill a glass with water at midnight during the festival and place curled strips of paper with the names of men and women inside, the next morning the least-curled paper is the name of your future husband or wife.

After a religious procession on Friday, the people follow through the town with a parade of decorated floats, drum-pounding bands, folk dancing, and plenty of wine. Fireworks sparkle each night. On Monday the fishing boats are blessed, and the streets are decorated with pictures in colored sawdust.

The Douro River Valley around Porto sees a folk-style pilgrimage to São Gonçalo at Amarante in June, and a three-day pilgrimage to Matosinhos at Whitsuntide. Thousands come from Galicia in Spain to Soajo to celebrate the festival of Senhora da Peñeda (sen-YOR-a da PEN-i-da), or Our Lady of Penitence, showing that the romaria is older than the frontier. The greatest pilgrimage of all, however, occurs in May or October to celebrate the visit of Our Lady of Fátima.

This pilgrimage is performed in remembrance of the six apparitions of the Virgin Mary to three peasant children in 1917. The children were shepherding their flock of sheep when a shining lady appeared to them. Their story was greeted with some doubt, but it gradually gained a following of thousands. Many people flock to Fátima every May and October to commemorate the apparitions.

ANCIENT ORIGINS OF CELEBRATIONS

Many festivals and fairs have their origins in pagan celebrations of springtime or harvest, old year or new. On the island of Madeira, Fim do Ano (fin do ANN-o), or the end of the old year, begins in the capital city of Funchal on December 8. Children sow seeds of wheat, corn, or lentils in moss or wet cotton fibers to sprout in time for Christmas. Each house is whitewashed and decorated. Honey and almond cakes are cooked, and spicy liqueurs are brewed. There is a replica of the Nativity scene in every church and home. The Portuguese share with the Chinese an affinity for gunpowder, so on the last night of the old year the country is ablaze with fireworks, spectacular in Madeira, and popular on the mainland as well. Then it is "Ano novo!" (ANN-o NOH-vo), or "Happy New Year," to all.

There is a Mimosa Festival in Viana do Castelo every Sunday in February, when the whole town is golden with blooming mimosa. Women in traditional dress sell handicrafts, and there is folk dancing in the streets. Carnival time in the cities falls on the Monday and Tuesday before Lent begins on Ash Wednesday. Huge, colorfully decorated floats trundle through the streets, and hotels hold dinner dances to enliven the night. Then arrives Easter, and the bullfighting season starts on Easter Sunday.

June, the midsummer month, is the time of the popular festivals of Saint António (Anthony), Saint João (John), and Saint Pedro (Peter). Song and dance resound all night during these festivals., The biggest fair of the year, featuring a wide and interesting array of local produce and handicrafts, is held during the festival of Saint Pedro at Sintra, near Lisbon. June is also the time when the Festas da Lisboa delights tourists and locals with many free exhibitions, concerts, and other cultural events sponsored by the city.

A young girl's face is painted for festivities in Loule, Portugal.

At the end of September, the whole country rejoices in the grape harvest. Then, on November 1, the people observe the Day of the Dead, particularly meaningful for the Portuguese, since on November 1, 1755, a great earthquake destroyed much of Lisbon. On this day, tombs are scrubbed clean, jars of flowers are brought in, and candles are lit.

The town of Ponte de Lima in the Minho has a special festival known as the Vaca das Cordas, which means "Cow of the Ropes." This festival has its roots in pre-Christian, classical mythology. Jupiter turned his lover Io into a cow because his mother refused to allow him to kidnap her. Io disappeared to Egypt, where she married the Egyptian god Osiris. The Egyptians worshipped the image of a cow to honor her and this was eventually brought over to Portugal.

In December, Christmas is celebrated with a midnight mass on Christmas Eve and traditional meals with family members.

INTERNET LINKS

www.fest300.com/festivals/festa-de-sao-joao
This site offers an in-depth description of the Festival of Saint John the Baptist in Porto, with photos and reviews.

www.me-n-youinportugal.com/index.php?blog&nid=31
This blog offers a rare look inside the "Cow of the Ropes" festival with great photos.

www.portugaldailyview.com/whats-new/fatima-a-how-to-guide-for-pilgrims
This site features a how-to guide for potential participants in the Fátima pilgrimage.

www.portugalvisitor.com/portugal-culture/portugal-festivals
This site lists famous (and not-so-famous) Portuguese festivals and pilgrimages by month.

FOOD

Meals featuring fresh seafood and vegetables are the highlight of the Portuguese table.

13

"Hunger is not only the best cook, but also the best physician."
–Traditional Portuguese proverb

MODERN PORTUGUESE COOKING owes a lot to its illustrious and adventuring past. From the lands they discovered, Portuguese traders returned home with new and unfamiliar spices like coriander, ginger, saffron, and paprika. From their voyages to India, the Portuguese came back with pepper, cinnamon, and curry powder—traditional Indian spices that are now staples in Portuguese cooking.

Following the marriage of King Charles II to Catherine of Bragança, the Portuguese princess brought tea, originally imported to Portugal from the Portuguese colony of Macau, to the English court. This is how tea first came to England. The Portuguese are also credited with introducing rice to Europe and refined sugar to Japan, when Portuguese trade ships first reached East Asia. Portuguese cuisine is also a major influence in the food of Macau, the Indian province of Goa, and, of course, Brazil.

Portuguese cooks sometimes use many spices at once and add cream and butter to make the food richer. Seafood, and especially cod, is a staple, and it can be served grilled, boiled, fried, stewed, or roasted. Most of the time, though, cod is served dried and salted—a tradition passed down from the earliest Portuguese cooks who had to make their meals last without refrigeration.

The best restaurants in the country are located in Lisbon, although delicious food can be found throughout Portugal. Tascas are small and simple restaurants that are often family-run, where the mother presides over the stove and the father waits on tables. These informal restaurants serve hearty meals and are staples of Portuguese social life. Often, portions are so large that you can order half-portions, even for adults. Many menus list the price of half-portions, usually at two-thirds of the full rate.

HABITS

Fish, fresh or dried, and many forms of shellfish are popular. But prices are rising, and poorer families make do with homegrown vegetables made spicy by the addition of a few slices of garlic-flavored sausage. The popularity of the cheap, backstreet tascas remains high. These simple food haunts often provide some of the best food in Portugal.

Portuguese cooking would be impossible without olive oil. The Portuguese pour it over potatoes and dried cod and cook with it most of the time. Although there are modern mechanical processes to create and refine the oil, traditional stone wheels are still used in rural parts of the country.

Most Portuguese blend their own coffee. Even a modest shop will offer a choice of fifteen to twenty different beans and roasts. A strong, dark cup of coffee, called a *bica* (BI-kah), is often drunk together with a glass of port. Tea is drunk, too, in the style that Catherine of Bragança introduced to her husband, King Charles II of England—so starting the English habit of taking afternoon tea. It is called *chá* (cha), copied from the Chinese word for tea—possibly the origin of the English "cup o' char," meaning "cup of tea."

SOUPS AND STEWS

Portuguese cuisine is famous for its filling stews and soups. Friendly arguments persist on what Portugal's national dish is, but a clear contender is *caldo verde* (KAL-do VAIR-di), a green soup made from thin shreds of tender, deep green cabbage.

The cook boils potatoes, onion, and garlic in stock and olive oil, then rolls cabbage leaves into a fat cigar shape and shaves off slices with a sharp knife. These are dropped into the soup only a minute or two before serving, along

Piri-piri (PI-ri PI-ri) sauce is a special Portuguese hot sauce and marinade made from a hot chili pepper called African bird's eye chili. This thin, bright red sauce is used in many Portuguese dishes, from chicken and shrimp piri-piri to fish stew and tacos. The sauce can be easily made with a blender or just shaken in a jar, and any kind of chili pepper can be substituted for the African bird's eye chili. Just add crushed chilies, lemon juice and peel, onion, salt, paprika, and oil together, and blend.

Piri means "pepper" in Swahili, and these hot chilies were discovered by the Portuguese in the fifteenth century when they sailed up the east coast of Africa. Coming in contact with the local Swahili-speaking population, they brought back barrels of chilies on their ships, which they used to spice up their food as well as for medicinal purposes. Once they arrived back on Portuguese soil, these sailors introduced the chilies to their families and friends, and the love of piri-piri on the Iberian Peninsula began.

with thin slices of smoked sausage. Cornbread is sometimes crumbled into the soup. The finished dish, served in a large bowl, is very thick and tasty, and is often eaten with a fork.

This caldo verde is the specialty of Minho in the north. So, too, is the shellfish *açorda* (ass-OR-da), a dish of softened bread with oil, garlic, and whatever mussels, clams, or prawns that were netted in the catch for that day. The bread is soaked in the shellfish stock, and this turns the soup into a filling dish that is sometimes served with chopped coriander.

Pigs are raised on the plains of the Alentejo, where the locals eat *sopa alentejana* (SOPP-a al-ENT-ish-AH-na), a soup of chopped bacon, smoked ham, coriander, and onions. This is served with a slice of bread that is topped with an egg poached in the hot soup.

SEAFOOD

Soups are memorable in Portugal, but fish is supreme. Bought at early-morning fish markets, the freshest fish and shellfish are stewed in a dark brown sauce (with cumin, chopped parsley, tomatoes, garlic, and onions) to

COD

There are, they say, 365 ways to cook cod. So popular is this fish that it is known as o fiel amigo *(oh FEE-al a-MEE-go), the faithful friend.* Bacalhau *(bok-kel-YOW) is dried cod, which has to be soaked in water overnight before it can be cooked. It used to be the poor person's staple and was cooked fresh, and often right after it was caught. Today it is more expensive. Portuguese shops even*

import dried cod from Norway to supply determined customers. Both fresh and frozen cod are often baked on top of newly sliced potatoes, over which garlic oil is liberally dribbled, and fresh parsley sprinkled. Sometimes the fish is flaked and mixed with potato salad, bits of onions, tiny bits of hardboiled egg, and lots of black olives and olive oil. And there is the tasty bolinhos de bacalhau *(bol-EEN-yohs de bok-kel-YOW), patties made from dried cod—never to be referred to as fish cakes!*

make *caldeirada* (kal-dey-RAH-da), the heavy-tasting fish stew served in every coastal town. Every seaside street has a vendor grilling sardines to sell as a tasty snack.

Sole, bass, red mullet, hake, swordfish, and squid are caught from the sea. From the freshwater rivers come lampreys, salmon, eels, and trout. The Portuguese never tire of their many-flavored fish dishes. And, to the surprise of foreigners, they drink red wine with their sardines and dried salted cod. They mix seafood with meat, too, cooking pork with clams and stuffing trout with smoked ham.

PORK AND POULTRY

Portugal is not a land for those who love steak. The lack of grazing land for cattle and the poor conditions in which sheep and goats are raised mean that more preparation time and effort are needed to make the tough meat more tender. Pigs abound in the cork-oak forests of Alentejo, and much of the pork is made into garlicky sausages or delicate smoked ham.

Regional dishes include Porto's *dobrada* (dob-RAH-da), tripe stewed with beans, chicken, pigs' trotters, and other ingredients; *carne de porco à alentejana* (KAR-ni da POR-ko a al-ENT-ish-AH-na), a classic meat dish of the Alentejo plains with chunks of pork seasoned in wine, coriander, and onions, and served with clams; *leitão* (lay-TAN), suckling pig served in the vineyards of Bairrada; *iscas* (ISS-kas), the pan-fried liver popular in Lisbon;

and *churrascos* (choo-RASS-kos), or chicken barbecues, brushed with piri-piri, a more modern habit that started in the Algarve.

Suckling pig is the specialty of the town of Mealhada in Beira Litoral, 12 miles (19 km) north of Coimbra. There are at least a dozen restaurants serving it.

Other meat dishes include partridges, pigeons, and quail, wherever these game birds can be found. Most dishes in Portugal are served with either rice or fried potatoes; salads usually include lettuce, watercress, tomato, and pimento.

CHEESE

Most cheeses in Portugal are made from sheep's milk, although hard, yellow goat cheese is made as well. In the villages, cheese is still squeezed in cheesecloth so that the whey drips out before it is left to dry and grow a thick rind. The result is often rock-hard and bun-shaped. It may be creamy smooth in taste, or dry and peppery, with the taste of the herbs that the sheep eat on the mountains. Soft cottage cheeses (such as those from Tomar and Azeitão) are moist and eaten sprinkled with pepper and salt. Restaurants often serve a portion of cheese as an appetizer or to freshen the palate between courses. The best cheese, it is said, comes from the Serra da Estrela.

DESSERTS

Common desserts are *crème caramel* (krem ka-RA-mel) with toffee-flavored sauce, and rice pudding served sweet and sprinkled with cinnamon. Cake and coffee shops do a brisk trade—and the Belém cake shop in Lisbon, built in 1837, still sells cakes baked in a special way and served hot with sugar and cinnamon.

Egg-based desserts were introduced to the country by the Moors and these recipes were then perfected by nuns in Portugal. Convents are often famous for making sweets such as the *ovos moles* (OH-vos MOH-les) made of egg yolk and sugar and molded into the shapes of shells and fish. Sometimes the egg yolk is soaked in sugar syrup or mixed with ground almonds; the

mixture is always formed into miniature shapes of fruits, birds, animals, or geometric designs and baked. Some sweets have curious names, such as *orelhas de abade* (O-REL-yas da a-BAH-di), or abbot's ears, and *barrigas de freiras* (ba-REE-gas de FREY-as), or nuns' bellies. Desserts are undeniably a definite treat in Portugal, and there is a wide and interesting variety of sweet and heavenly delights to choose from.

The Portuguese can choose from a variety of fruits, such as pears, oranges, plums, figs, and apricots. Grapes, of course, come in many varieties, too. From the Azores can be obtained pineapples; from Madeira, custard apples and passion fruit.

Delicate *ovos moles* are shaped into butterflies, flowers, fruits, and animals for spring.

Tradition says that port wine was "invented" by two young wine shippers from Liverpool. In the late seventeenth century, wines were brought to Porto in wineskins on the backs of mules. To preserve the wine during this rough treatment, one of the young men had the idea of adding some brandy and, so it is said, port wine was born. It is still sometimes called "the Englishman's wine."

Certainly trade in this wine resulted in the first firm links between Portugal and Britain. The British did not wish to lose their supplies of Porto's rich red or white wines. When British shippers, greedy for profit, started adding all sorts of colorings and additives, the Marquis de Pombal made laws to regulate production of the wine. Exact areas for the vineyards were demarcated and control placed totally under the Alto Douro Wine Company. Later, the amount of brandy added was also limited.

Some port wines are aged in wooden casks, while others are bottled and labeled with the year of vintage. The quality varies from year to year, and certain "vintage years" are much prized, fetching high prices. Most of the port lodges (some of which store wine dating back to 1811) are located across the river from Porto city. At the Port Wine Institute in Lisbon, several hundred varieties of port wait to be sampled.

WINE AND BEER

The famous wines of Portugal include Madeira, port, and several table wines. The pink, slightly sparkling Mateus Rosé has gained fame abroad, and its potbellied bottle now travels worldwide. This delicate wine is named after Vila Mateus, a curlicued Baroque palace located beside a geometrical lake amid vine-terraced hills in the Trás-os-Montes region.

Smooth, red wine is produced in the Algarve, and several areas around Lisbon also make wines, including a sweet dessert wine called Moscatel. The bulk of Portuguese wine comes from the Douro River Valley near Porto and the hills of the Minho. The vinho verde produced here is unique to Portugal. The name means "green wine," a reference to the young age of the grapes used and not the color of the wine.

Vinho verde has a slightly bubbly quality and the flavor varies from refreshingly fruity to very dry and tart. The white wine goes well with richly flavored fish dishes, and the red with thick soups or peppered pork. Clean and clear, vinho verde is allowed to ferment in the bottle, usually with a pinch of sugar added at the mouth of the bottle.

In one remote northern village, a most unusual wine is produced. In 1809, the villagers of Boticas buried their wine to hide it from the invading French armies. Dug up a year or two later, they found that the wine tasted even better. They continued with the custom, and to the wine was bestowed the name *vinho dos mortos* (VEEN-yo dos MOR-tos), or the wine of the dead.

Another famous wine is Madeira, named after the volcanic island where it is pressed and bottled. It is a fortified wine (given longer life by the addition of distilled alcohol) and has a unique, nutty flavor. There are four main textures of the wine: *sercial* (SIR-sial) and *verdelho* (vair-DEL-o), which are dry on the tongue; and *bual* (BOO-al) and *malmsey* (MARM-si), which are sweet and rich.

Apart from wine, there is also bottled and draught beer. Sagres is the most popular draught and is known as "imperial." Of course, the Portuguese also drink water. Tap water in the municipal areas is clean, but many people prefer bottled mineral spring water.

INTERNET LINKS

wine.about.com/od/fortifiedwines/a/Port.htm
Learn about the history and various types of port wine.

www.marthastewart.com/938401/emerils-favorite-portuguese-recipes
The well-known chef Emeril Lagasse shares his favorite Portuguese recipes.

OVOS MOLES DE AVEIRO (EGG YOLK CUSTARD)

8 egg yolks
1 ½ cups (340 grams) sugar
½ cup (80 g) rice flour
1 cup (235 milliliters) water

Pour sugar into a saucepan with ½ cup water. Allow the sugar to boil until it reaches 245°F (118°C) or has turned into an even, syrupy texture.

In a separate saucepan, dissolve the rice flour in ½ cup (118 mL) water.

Add the sugar syrup to this mixture and allow it to cook on low for five minutes. Then turn off the heat, let it cool for several minutes, and add in the egg yolks.

Once the egg yolks have been added to the mixture, you can turn on the heat to low again, and stir for another five minutes. Don't let the mixture boil, as it will thicken on its own.

Pour the custard into baking dishes and let cool.

SOPA DE ALHO COM BATATAS (GARLIC AND POTATO SOUP)

1 tablespoon (14 g) butter
2 garlic cloves, minced
2 chicken bouillon cubes
4 cups (940 mL) boiling water
1 cup (235 mL) milk
2 large potatoes, peeled, boiled and mashed
6 tablespoons (90 mL) cream
pinch of salt

In a saucepan, heat the butter and garlic on low heat.

Add boiling water and then bouillon cubes on medium heat and allow it to simmer for 10 minutes.

Remove the saucepan from the heat and add milk and potatoes. Stir until combined.

Then put the saucepan back on high heat until it boils.

After the soup boils, take it off the stove and add in the cream.

Flavor with salt if necessary.

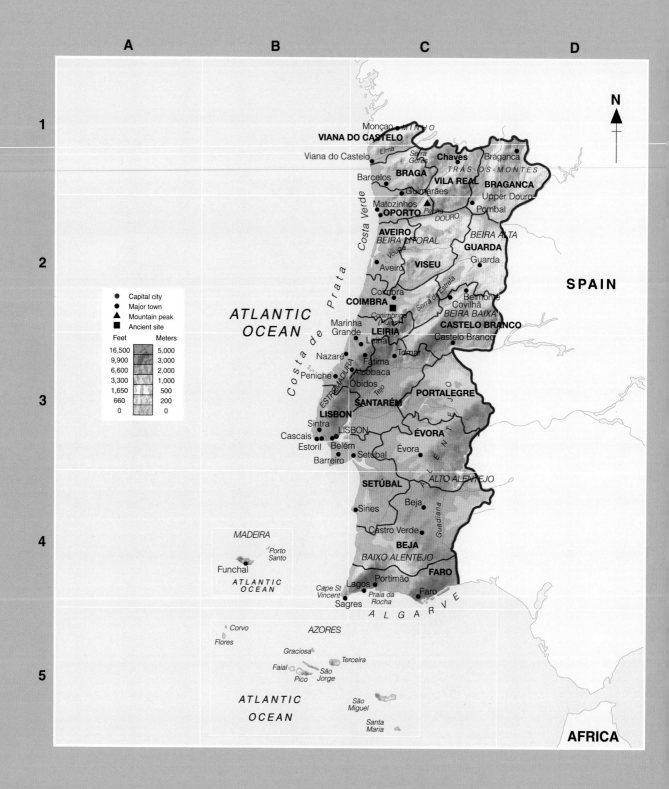

A   B   C   D

1

N

Monção
VIANA DO CASTELO
MINHO

Viana do Castelo
Lima
Serra
Gerês
Chaves
Braganca
TRÁS-OS-MONTES

Barcelos
BRAGA
VILA REAL
BRAGANÇA

Guimarães
Upper Douro
Matozinhos
Penha
Pombal
OPORTO
DOURO

AVEIRO
BEIRA ALTA
BEIRA LITORAL
Vouga
GUARDA

Aveiro
VISEU
Guarda

Coimbra
Belmonte
COIMBRA
Serra da Estrela
Covilhã
Conimbriga
(Ruins)
BEIRA BAIXA

2

SPAIN

**ATLANTIC
OCEAN**

Marinha
Grande
LEIRIA
CASTELO BRANCO

Leiria
Castelo Branco

Nazaré
Fátima
Tomar
Alcobaca

Peniche
Óbidos
Tejo

PORTALEGRE

SANTARÉM

LISBON
Sintra
LISBON
ÉVORA

Cascais
Estoril
Belém
Évora

Barreiro
Setúbal

ALTO ALENTEJO

SETÚBAL

Sines
Beja
Guadiana

Castro Verde
BEJA
BAIXO ALENTEJO

FARO

Portimão
Lagos
Faro
Cape St
Vincent
*Praia da
Rocha*
Sagres
A L G A R V E

3

4

5

● Capital city
● Major town
▲ Mountain peak
■ Ancient site

Feet	Meters
16,500	5,000
9,900	3,000
6,600	2,000
3,300	1,000
1,650	500
660	200
0	0

Costa Verde
Costa de Prata
Costa de Prata
ESTREMADURA

MADEIRA

Porto
Santo
Funchal
*ATLANTIC
OCEAN*

● Corvo
AZORES
Flores

Graciosa
Terceira
Faial
São
Jorge
Pico

São
Miguel

Santa
Maria

*ATLANTIC
OCEAN*

AFRICA

MAP OF PORTUGAL

ECONOMIC PORTUGAL

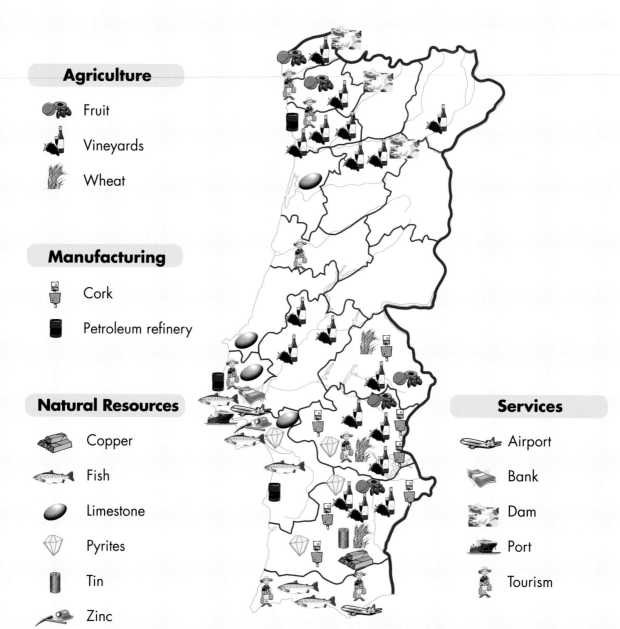

Agriculture
- Fruit
- Vineyards
- Wheat

Manufacturing
- Cork
- Petroleum refinery

Natural Resources
- Copper
- Fish
- Limestone
- Pyrites
- Tin
- Zinc

Services
- Airport
- Bank
- Dam
- Port
- Tourism

ABOUT THE ECONOMY

OVERVIEW

The past five years have been a difficult period for Portugal economically. Portugal proved to be susceptible to the European debt crisis that emerged in 2010, and in 2011, its leaders had to accept a €78 billion ($111 billion) debt package from the European Union and the International Monetary Fund. The unemployment rate in Portugal reached a record 17.7 percent in 2013 and the government was forced to implement austerity measures. However, 2014 marked a turnaround in Portugal's economy, and pre-crisis economic levels have been reached. The country exited the international bailout program in 2014 without having to ask for additional funds.

GROSS DOMESTIC PRODUCT (GDP)

$230 billion (2014)

GDP BY SECTOR

Agriculture 2.4 percent; industry 23.1 percent; services 74.4 percent

CURRENCY

1 euro (EUR) = 100 cents
Notes: 5, 10, 20, 50, 100, 200, 500 euros
Coins: 1, 2, 5, 10, 20, 50 cents; 1, 2 euros
USD 1 = EUR 0.88 (October 2015)

INFLATION RATE

0.9 percent

WORKFORCE

5.2 million

UNEMPLOYMENT RATE

12.4 percent (2015)

MAIN INDUSTRIES

Textiles, metalworking, oil refining, chemicals, fish canning, electronics and communications equipment, rail transportation equipment, aerospace equipment, ship construction and refurbishment, tourism

AGRICULTURAL PRODUCTS

Wood, cork, wine, olives

MAIN IMPORTS

Machinery and transportation equipment, chemicals, petroleum, textiles, agricultural products

MAIN EXPORTS

Clothing and footwear, machinery, chemicals, cork and paper products, hides

TRADE PARTNERS

Spain, France, Germany, United Kingdom, United States, Italy, Belgium, Netherlands

REGIONAL/INTERNATIONAL MEMBERSHIP

European Union, United Nations, North Atlantic Treaty Organization. Portugal is also party to numerous environmental treaties and protocols.

CULTURAL PORTUGAL

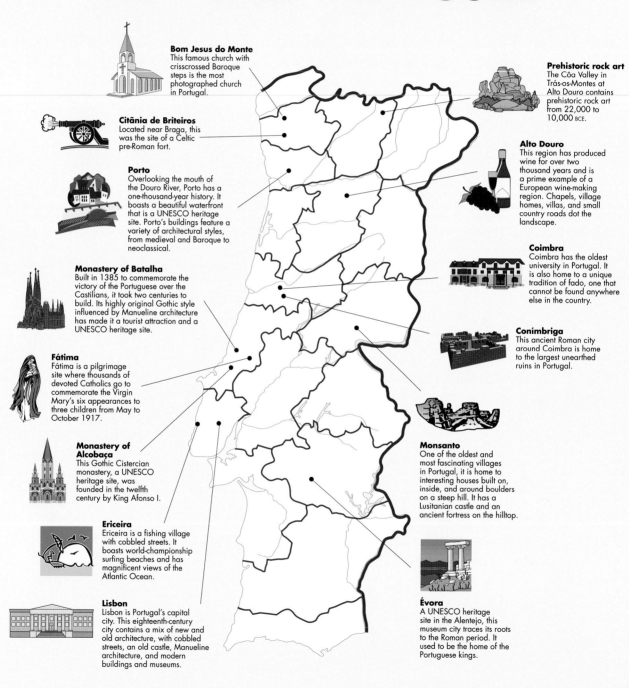

Bom Jesus do Monte
This famous church with crisscrossed Baroque steps is the most photographed church in Portugal.

Prehistoric rock art
The Côa Valley in Trás-os-Montes at Alto Douro contains prehistoric rock art from 22,000 to 10,000 BCE.

Citânia de Briteiros
Located near Braga, this was the site of a Celtic pre-Roman fort.

Alto Douro
This region has produced wine for over two thousand years and is a prime example of a European wine-making region. Chapels, village homes, villas, and small country roads dot the landscape.

Porto
Overlooking the mouth of the Douro River, Porto has a one-thousand-year history. It boasts a beautiful waterfront that is a UNESCO heritage site. Porto's buildings feature a variety of architectural styles, from medieval and Baroque to neoclassical.

Coimbra
Coimbra has the oldest university in Portugal. It is also home to a unique tradition of fado, one that cannot be found anywhere else in the country.

Monastery of Batalha
Built in 1385 to commemorate the victory of the Portuguese over the Castilians, it took two centuries to build. Its highly original Gothic style influenced by Manueline architecture has made it a tourist attraction and a UNESCO heritage site.

Conímbriga
This ancient Roman city around Coimbra is home to the largest unearthed ruins in Portugal.

Fátima
Fátima is a pilgrimage site where thousands of devoted Catholics go to commemorate the Virgin Mary's six appearances to three children from May to October 1917.

Monsanto
One of the oldest and most fascinating villages in Portugal, it is home to interesting houses built on, inside, and around boulders on a steep hill. It has a Lusitanian castle and an ancient fortress on the hilltop.

Monastery of Alcobaça
This Gothic Cistercian monastery, a UNESCO heritage site, was founded in the twelfth century by King Afonso I.

Ericeira
Ericeira is a fishing village with cobbled streets. It boasts world-championship surfing beaches and has magnificent views of the Atlantic Ocean.

Évora
A UNESCO heritage site in the Alentejo, this museum city traces its roots to the Roman period. It used to be the home of the Portuguese kings.

Lisbon
Lisbon is Portugal's capital city. This eighteenth-century city contains a mix of new and old architecture, with cobbled streets, an old castle, Manueline architecture, and modern buildings and museums.

ABOUT THE CULTURE

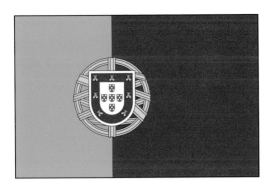

OFFICIAL NAME
Portuguese Republic

CAPITAL
Lisbon

GOVERNMENT TYPE
Parliamentary democracy

NATIONAL FLAG
Green and red background with the country's coat of arms.

NATIONAL ANTHEM
"A Portuguesa." Composed in 1891 and adopted by the republic in 1911. Music by Alfredo Keil; lyrics by Henrique Lopes de Mendonça.

POPULATION
10,561,614 (2011)

LIFE EXPECTANCY
average: 80.37 years, men: 77; women: 84

LITERACY RATE
95.4 percent; male 97 percent, female 94 percent

ETHNIC GROUPS
Portuguese, Roma, Galician, Mirandesa, Cape Verdian, North African Arab, Brazilian, Angolan, Guinea-Bisau, Goanese

OFFICIAL LANGUAGES
Portuguese, Mirandese

RELIGIOUS GROUPS
Roman Catholic, Protestant, Muslim, Hindu, and Jewish

PUBLIC HOLIDAYS
New Years' Day (January 1), Shrove Tuesday (February/March), Good Friday (March/April), Liberty Day (April 25), Labor Day (May 1), Corpus Christi (May/June), Portugal Day (June 10), Feast of the Assumption (August 15), Republic Day (October 5), All Saints' Day (November 1), Independence from Spain (December 1), Immaculate Conception (December 8), Christmas Day (December 25).

TIMELINE

IN PORTUGAL	IN THE WORLD
	753 BCE Rome is founded.
210–60 BCE The Romans conquer the Lusitanians.	**116–117 CE** The Roman Empire reaches its greatest extent, under Emperor Trajan (reigned 98–117).
711–716 CE Moors invade the Iberian Peninsula.	
	1000 The Chinese perfect gunpowder and begin to use it in warfare.
1139 Afonso Henriques I becomes the first king.	
1143 Castile recognizes Portugal as an independent nation.	
1499 Explorer Vasco da Gama reaches India.	**1530** Beginning of transatlantic slave trade organized by the Portuguese in Africa.
1572 Luís Vaz de Camões publishes the *Lusiads*.	**1558–1603** Reign of Elizabeth I of England.
	1620 Pilgrims sail the *Mayflower* to America.
1755 An earthquake destroys Lisbon.	**1776** US Declaration of Independence signed.
	1789–1799 The French Revolution.
1807 Napoleon's troops invade Portugal.	**1861** The US Civil War begins.
	1869 The Suez Canal is opened.
	1914 World War I begins.
1932 António de Oliveira Salazar becomes the prime minister of Portugal.	**1939** World War II begins.
	1945 The United States drops atomic bombs on Hiroshima and Nagasaki.
	1949 NATO is formed.
	1957 The Russians launch *Sputnik 1*.

IN PORTUGAL		IN THE WORLD
		1966–1969
		The Chinese Cultural Revolution.
1970		
Salazar dies.		
1974		
Revolution of the Carnations.		
1975		
Portugal decolonizes its remaining empire in Africa; Macau remains a Portuguese colony.		
1983		
Mário Soares becomes prime minister.		**1986**
		Nuclear power disaster at Chernobyl in Ukraine.
		1991
1996		Breakup of the Soviet Union.
Jorge Sampaió becomes president.		**1997**
1999		Hong Kong is returned to China.
Macau is handed over to China.		
2001		**2001**
Jorge Sampaió is reelected as president.		Terrorists crash planes in New York,
2002		Washington, DC, and Pennsylvania.
Social democrats win the elections. Durao Barroso becomes prime minister.		
2003		**2003**
Portugal hosts the Iraq War Conference.		War in Iraq.
2004		
Barroso resigns as prime minister. Pedro Santana Lopes takes over.		
2005		
Socialists win general elections. José Sócrates becomes prime minister.		
2010		**2010**
A law allowing same-sex marriage is approved by President Cavaco Silva. Parliament passes austerity budget due to high debt levels.		European debt crisis begins.
2011		**2011**
The EU and the IMF agree to a €78 billion bailout for Portugal.		Arab Spring uprisings begin in Tunisia, Egypt, and Libya, followed by the Syrian civil war.
2014		**2014**
Portugal exits international bailout without seeking additional credit.		ISIS (The Islamic State of Iraq and Syria) begins attacks in northern Iraq and Syria.

GLOSSARY

Algarve
Coastal region in the south of Portugal.

azulejos (ah-zoo-LAY-shoss)
Glazed ceramic tiles that adorn buildings throughout Portugal.

bacalhau (borh-kerhl-YAO)
Dried salted cod.

bica (BI-kah)
A type of strong, dark coffee served in a demitasse-style cup.

caldo verde (KAL-do VAIR-di)
Green soup made from cabbage and potatoes.

caravel
A speedy 60-foot (18-meter) ship with a triangular rig, designed by Prince Henry's navigation experts.

cork oak
The tree from which cork bark is obtained.

escudo (ess-KOO-do)
Portugal's former unit of currency.

fadista (fa-DIS-ta)
A folksinger.

fado (FAH-doh)
Nostalgic folksongs.

festa (FES-ta)
A celebration.

Manueline
An exquisite and elaborate nautical style of architecture inspired by Portuguese exploration of the world. It was named after King Manuel I of Portugal who reigned from 1495 to 1521.

namoro (NAM-o-ro)
Formal engagement period preceding marriage.

port
A sweet, rich wine made from grapes grown in the Douro Valley.

pousadas (poo-SAH-das)
Historic buildings that have been turned into state guesthouses or inns.

retornados (re-tor-NAH-dose)
Portuguese who have emigrated but are forced by circumstances to return to their homeland.

romaria (roh-MAH-ri-a)
A pilgrimage.

saudade (sow-DAH-de)
A feeling of homesickness, longing, or nostalgia.

vinho verde (VEEN-yo VAIR-di)
Young, green wine from Northwest Portugal.

BOOKS

Ali, Monica. *Alentejo Blue.* New York: Scribner, 2006.

Camões, Luis Vaz de. *The Lusiads.* Translated by Landeg White. Oxford, UK: Oxford Paperbacks, 2008.

Coelho, Paulo. *Aleph.* Translated by Margaret Jull Costa. New York: Random House, 2011.

Disney, A.R. *A History of Portugal and the Portuguese Empire, Vol. 1: From Beginnings to 1807.* Cambridge, UK: Cambridge University Press, 2009.

Johnston, Francis. *Fatima: The Great Sign.* Charlotte, NC: TAN Books, 2015.

Lobo Antunes, António. *The Fat Man and Infinity: And Other Writings.* Translated by Margaret Jull Costa. New York: W.W. Norton & Company, 2009.

Mendes, George, and Genevieve Ko. *My Portugal: Recipes and Stories.* New York: Stewart, Tabori, and Chang, 2014.

Ortins, Patuleia Ana. *Authentic Portuguese Cooking: More Than 185 Classic Mediterranean-Stlye Recipes of the Azores, Madeira and Continental Portugal.* Salem, MA: Page Street Publishing, 2015.

Pessoa, Fernando. *A Little Larger Than the Entire Universe: Selected Poems.* Translated by Richard Zenith. New York: Penguin Classics, 2006.

Pessoa, Fernando. *Philosophical Essays: A Critical Edition.* Edited by Nuno Ribeiro. New York: Contra Mundum Press, 2012.

Santos, José Rodrigues dos. *The Einstein Enigma.* Translated by Lisa Carter. New York: William Morrow, 2011.

Zweig, Stefan. *Magellan.* Translated by Cedar Paul and Eden Paul. London: Pushkin Press, 2012.

WEBSITES

About Manoel de Oliveria. www.imdb.com/name/nm0210701

BBC News Country Profile: Portugal. www.bbc.com/news/world-europe-17758217

Central Intelligence Agency World Factbook: Portugal. https://www.cia.gov/library/publications/the-world-factbook/geos/po.html

The Economist Country Briefings: Portugal. www.economist.com/countries/Portugal

National and Natural Parks of Portugal. www.manorhouses.com/parks/index.html

Portuguese Culture Center. www.portugueseculturalcenter.com

The Portuguese News (Online English Newspaper). www.theportugalnews.com

Virtual Portugal. www.portugalvirtual.pt/index.html

MUSIC

The Art of Amália Rodrigues. Blue Note Records, 1998.

Mariza, Fado Em Mim. Times Square Records, 2002.

Aurea. Essência. União Lisboa, 2015.

BIBLIOGRAPHY

About Manoel de Oliveria. http://www.imdb.com/name/nm0210701.

Amorim CorkFacts. http://www.amorimcork.com/en.

BBC News. http://www.bbc.co.uk.

Brown, Jules, Mark Ellingham, John Fisher, and Matthew Hancock. *The Rough Guide to Portugal.* 14th revised edition. New York, NY: Rough Guides, 2013.

Central Intelligence Agency World Factbook: Portugal. https://www.cia.gov/library/publications/the-world-factbook/geos/po.html

Eironline (European Industrial relations observatory). http://www.eurofound.europa.eu/observatories/eurwork.

European Commission. *Country Report: Portugal 2015.* Brussels, 2015.

European Foundation for the Improvement of Living and Working Conditions. http://www.eurofound.europa.eu.

Gray, Lila Ellen. *Fado Resounding: Affective Politics and Urban Life.* Durham, NC: Duke University Press, 2013.

Hatton, Barry. *The Portuguese: A Modern History.* Northampton, MA: Interlink Publishing Group, 2011.

Herbach, Andy. *Eating and Drinking in Spain and Portugal.* Cold Spring Harbor, NY: Open Road, 2014.

OECD Secretariat. *Better Policies Portugal: Deepening Structural Reform to Support Growth and Competitiveness.* Paris: Organisation for Economic Co-operation and Development, 2014.

Porto express—Recipes. http://www.portoexpress.com/pastrecipes.htm.

The Portuguese News (online English newspaper). http://www.theportugalnews.com.

Stephens, H. Morse. *A Short History of Portugal: From the Earliest Times to the 19th Century.* San Diego, CA: Didactic Press, 2015.

Wheeler, Douglas I. and Walter C. Opello Jr.. *Historical Dictionary of Portugal.* 3rd edition. Lanham, MD: Scarecrow Press, 2010.

INDEX

INDEX